Vocational Business

5

Finance

Keith Brumfitt, & Jane Jones

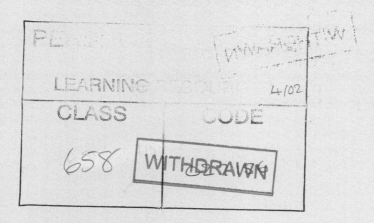

Series Editor: Keith Brumfitt

Published in 2001 by:
Nelson Thornes Ltd
Delta Place
27 Bath Road
CHELTENHAM
GL53 7TH
United Kingdom

01 02 03 04 05 / 10 9 8 7 6 5 4 3 2 1

A catalogue record for this book is available from the British Library

ISBN 0 748 6363 5

Illustrations by Oxford Designers and Illustrators

Page make-up and illustrations by GreenGate Publishing Services, Tonbridge, Kent

Printed and bound in Italy by Stige

Contents

Introduction to Vocational Business series   iv

Titles in the Vocational Business series   iv

Acknowledgements   iv

Introduction   1

Financial information   1

Financial documents   9

Book-keeping   18

Has a profit been made?   32

Key ratios   36

Measuring solvency   41

The shareholder perspective   43

Financial information and stakeholders   47

Limitations of ratios   52

Budgeting   53

Cash flow and working capital   58

Profit or cash   62

Index   68

Introduction to Vocational Business series

This textbook is one of a series of six covering the core areas of business studies. Each book focuses on vocational aspects of business, rather than theoretical models, allowing the reader to understand how businesses operate. To complement this vocational focus, each book contains a range of case studies illustrating how businesses respond to internal and external changes.

The textbooks are designed to support students taking a range of business courses. While each is free standing, containing the essential knowledge required by the various syllabuses and course requirements, together they provide a comprehensive coverage of the issues facing both large and small businesses in today's competitive environment.

Titles in the series

Book 1   **Business at Work**
Book 2   **The Competitive Business Environment**
Book 3   **Marketing**
Book 4   **Human Resources**
Book 5   **Finance**
Book 6   **Business Planning**

Acknowledgements

The authors and publishers would like to thank the following people and organisations for permission to reproduce photographs and other material:
Astra Zeneca UK Ltd; Cadbury Schweppes plc; Next plc; PizzaExpress plc; Diana Roberts; Thorntons plc, Charles Winpenny/Cornwall Cam.

Every effort has been made to contact copright holders, and we apologise if any have been overlooked.

|Finance

Introduction

In this book you will find out how businesses manage their finances and about the important indicators of their financial health. You will need to understand the processes of financial monitoring and forecasting and the routine aspects of managing business finance. You will learn how to record financial information and how to interpret this information to make judgements about the effectiveness of business. You will also find out about the importance of financial management in fulfilling the aims of people with a stake in the business.

| Financial information

What are financial records?

The purpose of business is to combine scarce resources – materials, equipment and people – so that the value of outputs adequately exceeds the cost of inputs. It's worth thinking carefully about this statement: it

Value added, page 32

applies equally to manufacturing and services, to small and large firms. There are no exceptions. Even charities must ensure that their costs are only a small fraction of the income that they can attract.

To make possible specialisation and exchange, almost all business transactions are expressed in terms of money. This means that money is the 'language' of markets and the whole process of adding value. It is the 'unit of account' and means that firms keep records of their transactions in terms of money. Put another way, every business decision or event that involves the use of resources leaves a financial record or 'imprint' in the firm's accounts.

What exactly are accounts? You may have come across the idea of 'accountability' or 'being held to account'. Even the idea that someone should 'account for themselves' conveys the essential meaning. 'Accounting' is giving an 'account' of the firm's activities in the language of money.

Making a profit

On 1 January a trader buys 1,000 watches at £8.00 each and after a mark up of 50 per cent has sold them all by 31 January at £12 each:

	£
Sales revenue (1,000 × £12)	12,000
Cost of goods sold (1,000 × £8)	8,000
Profit (1,000 × £4)	4,000

This is a simple account of the trader's business transactions for January. Every business experiences and records very different kinds of financial events. Rents and rates are paid. Stock is purchased. Debts are incurred. Wages are paid. Equipment is bought. Loans are obtained. In a large firm, thousands of transactions like this occur every day. Every one of them leaves a record on the accounts. In this way financial records are a coded description of the real events that make up business activity. The code is not difficult to learn but it is very revealing.

What does financial information tell us?

Like the 'black box' flight recorder on an aircraft, the financial records generated by business activity invariably tell a story. Partly it is a story about costs and sales revenues (resources going out and resources coming in). This two-way process is the motor under every business. Financial information allows the progress of the enterprise to be monitored and its underlying profitability to be assessed, but it also enables a whole network of important questions to be asked. For example:

- What is the value of the firm's assets (things of value)?
- How does the performance of the business compare with previous years?
- How is the value and volume of sales changing?
- Are costs above or below those of competitors?
- Have labour costs risen or fallen?
- What savings have been achieved through investment? (e.g. by buying new machinery)
- How much has loan finance cost in interest?

The answers to such questions guide managers in recognising and sorting out difficulties. A business with declining sales or rising costs may face serious problems unless effective action is taken to reverse the trend. Equally a firm with increasing sales might need funds to expand or a firm with lower costs than those of competitors might explore new marketing opportunities.

The other story told by financial information is about people. This may seem surprising as business finance is often seen as 'dry' or 'technical'. But exploration of financial data often uncovers a human drama. Failure of a new product may cost the manager his or her job. Rising costs or an inability to reduce costs might spell redundancies for some of the workforce.

CTIVITY

Next

Back in the 1980s – although there were four other directors – George Davies *was* Next. As Chief Executive, his talent, energy and personality swept the firm forward. And the pace of expansion was manic. Soon Davies had launched Next for Men and was planning to take Next's reputation for style and value in a range of new directions. The result was Next Interiors, Next Accessories, Next Cosmetics, Next Lingerie, Next Florist, Next Café and more. Sales and profits soared.

In 1986 Next entered a £300 million merger with Gratton's, a leading mail order firm and a year later spent £340 million on the takeover of Combined English Stores. What started as an inspirational but fairly small firm had mushroomed by the late 1980s into a sprawling business empire. But when the magic finally faltered, it was inevitable that George Davies would be in the firing line.

His downfall was swift and brutal. As it became clear that Next was facing real difficulties, his future directors planned a coup. Almost without warning George Davies was fired.

In reality, Next was heading into a nose-dive. The company had borrowed far too much money and bought vast amounts of commercial property. Rising interest rates, falling property values and a deep

Figure 5.1

recession nearly bankrupted Next. By 1990, as one store manager put it: 'We didn't know if we'd be opening again on Monday.'

Table 5.1 *Financial information 1985–89 (£m)*

Year	1985	1986	1987	1988	1989
Sales	164	372	862	1,210	1,028
Costs	144	330	770	1,148	1,075

Source: Next Annual Report and Accounts, 1985–90

The costs shown above include all costs that should be deducted in calculating profit before tax.

Due to changes in Next's accounting period, some information is based on author estimates.

Tasks

1 Graph sales and costs data for the period. What features do you notice?
2 How did the firm's profit margin (Profit before tax/Sales) vary over these years?

Next's fortunes changed during the 1990s and once again it became a successful fashion retailer.

 Profit margin, page 38

How is financial information collected?

Look inside the last plastic bag that you were handed in a shop and the odds are that it contains a receipt. This is a record of your transaction with that company. All firms keep a record of sales, broken down by business unit and dates. Records are also kept of costs so that it is possible to track the firm's use of resources and calculate its profit. This is essential to business management and enables a firm to prepare accounts and assess its tax liability.

The detailed information collected from day-to-day transactions builds up over time to give a larger picture. For example, answers can be found to such questions as:

- What was the volume and value of sales last year?
- What was the average value of sales in the London area each month?
- At what rate are sales rising or falling?

This information will be broken down by division, branch, product or other useful criteria.

A CTIVITY

1 In the table below, identify which paper has the best and worst performance in terms of changes in sales revenue.
2 If you were trying to assess the sales performance of *The Mirror*, what other data would you want?

Table 5.2 *Daily newspaper sales (circulation in 000s)*

	1995 Circulation	Price (p)	2000 Circulation	Price (p)
The Sun	3,679	24	4,016	30
The Mirror	2,919	25	2,443	32
Daily Mail	1,702	32	2,074	40
Daily Express	1,542	30	1,220	35
The Times	396	30	738	40
The Independent	383	35	272	45

Source: Marketing Pocket Book 2001 (NTC Publications)

In some small enterprises, financial information is still recorded manually and exists as a written record. But most firms – and all major companies – now use electronic computerised systems. For example, EPOS (electronic point-of-sales) systems scan goods and feed data into computerised accounting and stock control programs. Computerisation has brought a revolution in access to financial information. Far more closely defined and up-to-date data is now available at lower cost than ever before. For example, a major chain store will be able immediately to analyse sales of any product line at any branch for any week or day. Increasingly financial information is becoming available in real time and not historic time.

This makes managing business more like driving a car than sitting on the bridge of an ocean liner. No longer need managers find that they have long since sailed past the evidence of market change or that changing direction takes longer than the lifespan of the opportunity identified. Running today's business enterprise is rather like driving round the M25: quick reactions are at a premium.

ISBN 0-7487-6363-5

Figure 5.2 *Bar code*

ASE STUDY

In the driving seat

You are sitting in the driving seat of an expensive car. On the road ahead you need to make good time but equally it is essential to avoid accidents. There are a number of instruments on the dashboard to help you. The speedometer, rev counter, clock and fuel gauge all provide useful information. This data will combine with your skill as a driver in helping you to reach your target destination at the time agreed. The challenge of financial management is rather similar.

Key term

Real time information means data that is accurate at the present time and is updated continuously. This usually involves electronic transmission and presentation. Real time information is in contrast to historic data that was accurate at an earlier date and is usually printed.

Key terms

Opportunity cost is the cost of giving something up, e.g. by working late an employee gives up the opportunity to spend time with his family. This lost opportunity can be given a financial value which is called the opportunity cost.
Management by exception and **the principle of exception** refer to the idea that a manager's attention should be focused not on variables that are behaving normally but on those that are behaving abnormally or are out of line with targets. Exceptions to what is expected can then be discovered and analysed early, thus enabling necessary decisions to be made promptly.

Making information valuable

Information is never free. There is always some cost in collecting and communicating the information, even if it is only the opportunity cost of people's time. Although computer power has greatly reduced costs, the real value of information depends on its selection, presentation and communication. The old saying 'garbage in, garbage out' is a relevant reminder that computerised information services are only as useful as their systems and software allow.

Like any product, financial information is subject to the principles of added value. Raw and undigested information has little use: it is just a raw material. Once sorted, shaped, carefully presented and directed to the right place at the right time, it becomes highly valuable.

It is all too easy for electronic systems to generate huge amounts of poorly directed, low value information. One side of A4 paper or one screen page containing key financial data is worth far more than very many files filled with potentially valuable but unedited information.

One important way in which financial information can be sharpened in its impact is by highlighting exceptions from the 'norm' (normal occurrences). Think of a retail chain such as WH Smith. Most of the time, sales of most products should be roughly in line with expectations. Then suppose that one store begins seriously to underperform. Or perhaps within one store, sales of fountain pens fall. It is exceptions like these that can be highlighted in the flow of information and brought to the attention of relevant managers. They can then investigate the cause of the problem (or opportunity, when events are unexpectedly favourable). In this case the underperforming store may be facing unexpected local competition. And the fall in fountain pen sales at another store may be due to inexperienced or untrained sales staff. In this way, using the principle of exception, financial information can bring about appropriate management action.

Accounting requirements

Keeping accounts is not an optional activity. Even the smallest business needs to keep accounts so that a proper return can be made to the Inland Revenue. Companies are legally required to keep and produce accounts according to the Companies Acts 1985 and 1989. These are filed with Companies House in Cardiff and are open to inspection by any member of the public on payment of a small fee. Larger public companies must publish more detailed accounts in their formal Annual Reports and Accounts which are available to everyone free of charge.

There are three basic accounting statements derived from business records:

- the Profit and Loss Account which records the total value of sales and shows the successive deductions of costs, interest and taxation that give rise to profit or loss
- the balance sheet which indicates the sources of the firm's finance and how it is currently used

- the cash flow statement which shows all flows of cash into and out of the firm.

Notice that the profit and loss account and the cash flow statement relate to the preceding year whereas the balance sheet relates to one date at the end of that year.

The exact requirements of the law vary according to the size and type of company. Private companies need only submit a balance sheet and a profit and loss account. If they are small or medium-sized, then only 'abbreviated' accounts (less detailed) are necessary although full accounts must still be produced for shareholders. Public companies must publish all their primary accounting statements and must use an approved format.

Understanding accounts

What is accounting?

Accounting means keeping records of how an organisation uses its resources. These records are expressed in terms of money as a standard unit of account.

Accountants

Accountants must have specialist qualifications and normally belong to one of the relevant professional bodies:

- Institute of Chartered Accountants
- Chartered Association of Certified Accountants
- Institute of Cost and Management Accountants
- Chartered Institute of Public Finance and Accountancy.

Until 1990 these organisations were represented by the Accounting Standards Committee which issued SSAPs (Statements of Standard Accounting Practice). These 'rules' had no legal force but were generally accepted and designed to ensure reasonable consistency in the work of the profession.

Since 1990 the Financial Reporting Council (FRC) has had full legal responsibility for accounting standards. Detailed work is carried out by the Accounting Standards Board (ASB) and its decisions have the force of law. Companies failing to comply with ASB standards may face the Financial Reporting Review Panel which can require revised accounts. The ASB has adopted all active SSAPs and has also issued its own new standards called Financial Reporting Standards (FRSs). The Companies Act 1989 defined accounting standards and a legal requirement that they be observed.

Throughout the 1990s there was much discussion about accounting standards and the level of disclosure (i.e. the extent to which companies must make accounting information public). There also continues to be much debate about the rights of shareholders and the behaviour of institutional investors such as pension funds.

There are two types of accounting:

- ■ **Financial accounting** aims to record accurately financial events. Its focus is on offering a 'true and fair view' of the organisation's affairs. Its product is the periodic published accounting that meet external obligations.

- ■ **Management accounting** aims to use accounting data for the guidance of management decision-making. The focus is on internal use as a financial 'intelligence system'. The product of management accounting is data about every aspect of sales, costs, the sources and uses of funds and the flow of cash through the business. For example, the management accountant might be required to calculate unit costs as an input to the pricing decision.

Key terms

Financial accounting involves the collection, analysis and presentation of data to make possible the construction of legally required accounting statements such as the balance sheet and the profit and loss account.
Management accounting involves designing the flow of accounting data so that it has maximum value in assisting the process of management and decision-making.

Key terms

Corporate governance is the procedures, standards and culture that represent the way a company conducts its affairs.

Non-executive directors are part-time members of a company's board who do not take part in day-to-day management but play a supervisory role in ensuring that shareholders' interests are properly represented.

The **chairman** of a company runs meetings of the board of directors and takes responsibility for long-term aims and objectives.

The **chief executive** (or managing director) takes the leading role in shaping and implementing a strategy that is designed to fulfil agreed aims and objectives.

In 1998 the Hampel Committee reported on corporate governance which refers to the structure of power and responsibility in public companies. The committee adopted the Stock Exchange's Combined Code, incorporating two earlier reports. A key role was recommended for non-executive directors – part-time members of the board who do not have any day-to-day management responsibilities. They were expected to provide useful advice and to guard shareholders' interests. Companies were also advised to split the roles of chairman and chief executive so as to avoid excessive concentration of power. This recommendation has generally been adopted.

Basic accounting concepts

There are a number of key ideas in accounting that exist to ensure that all accounts give a 'true and fair view' of an organisation's financial affairs.

Figure 5.3

CASE STUDY

The Big Star

Table 5.3

1 Separate entity	
At law a company is a legal 'person' with an existence separate from other companies or individuals. The affairs of the company must not get tangled with the private affairs of directors or shareholders.	**The Big Star Ltd.** This is a recently established chain of fashion jewellery shops in the Manchester area. Kerrie Barker, one of the owner directors, knows that she must keep her private belongings separate from the company's property.
2 Consistency	
This means that similar items or situations must be treated consistently over time, i.e. in the same way. It ensures that one year's data is comparable with another.	Kerrie is careful to measure and value all costs and revenues in the same way. This ensures that recorded profits will be comparable from one period to another.
3 Prudence or Conservatism	
Accountants always 'look on the black side'! The good news of profits is only recognised when	Nicky Harper is the Accounts Manager for Big Star Ltd. She only records profits when they

money is received. The bad news of any losses will be estimated as soon as it becomes likely.

are actually realised through real sales. But she always makes a 'worst case' estimate of losses on slow-selling stock.

4 Matching

The aim is to match all revenues with their coresponding costs. The sales recorded in an accounting period are matched *not* with all costs in the same period but with *those costs that relate to those sales*.

When Jon Glover bought a large consignment of Indian jewellery in November, the Cost of Goods Sold for the year only included items sold by 31 December. The remainder of the cost was carried over to the following year.

5 Double entry

Every financial transaction has two sides. A change in the use of funds must mean an increase under one heading and a decrease under another. Obtaining new funds must mean an increase in a source of funds and an increase in a use of funds.

Nicky enters the value of the consignment as an *increase* in 'stock' and enters the expenditure as a decrease in 'cash'. In this way she has made a double entry.

▎Financial documents

Why keep records?

Business management is only possible with information about the firm's resources and the flows of resources resulting from the business's activities. Collecting information depends on keeping accurate financial records. This is a legal requirement so that taxation can be assessed and – in the case of companies – necessary information can be made available to outsiders.

Every business is involved in a constant stream of:
- buying and selling goods and services
- making and receiving payments.

These events are recorded through the use of financial documents. Although these are increasingly likely to be processed in an electronic format, the 'documents' are still required and often appear as hard copy at some stage in their use.

Figure 5.4

A list like this grows very quickly even in a small business. The owners would soon face chaos if proper records were not kept of the different kinds of financial events occurring, such as:

- sales and purchases of goods and services
- incomings and outgoings of money
- payment of wages and movement of stock.

In all cases the business needs well kept financial records to ensure that the Inland Revenue can assess any tax due and to satisfy HM Customs and Excise that VAT has been correctly administered. If the enterprise is a limited company, then an external accountant will need access to all financial data so that the annual audit of the accounts can be made.

Finally most firms will sometimes need to arrange bank loans or a bank overdraft. Again, financial records will be important in supporting the firm's application to borrow.

Key term

An **annual audit** of an firm's accounts is an external check on the data to make sure that it represents 'a true and fair view' of the organisation's affairs.

Key financial documents

All business transactions take place in a market and involve an exchange between a buyer and a seller. Each transaction entails communication between buyer and seller and we can consider this as the evidence – rather like footprints – that the transaction leaves behind. Sometimes the interaction between buyer and seller is brief and simple. For example, you buy a box of chocolates and receive a till receipt. As buyer you have a paper record that you may or may not wish to keep. The seller has an electronic record of the sale and increasingly a signal to their stock control system that one more item has been sold. But when a larger transaction takes place – typically between two firms – a longer sequence of communication takes place.

CASE STUDY

JungleBox – a sweet sensation

Nick and Debbie Kerslake own JungleWorld, a theme park that promises visitors 'all the excitement of life in the jungle'. Families and children are offered a wide range of attractions with an expanding gift shop where the admission fees are also paid.

Debbie wants to launch boxes of exciting sweets, imaginatively packaged and under the name 'JungleBox'. She's aware of a possible supplier called Sweet Sensation. The first step is to find out about products and prices. Debbie may send letters of enquiry to Sweet Sensation and other suppliers of confectionery. In return she may expect to receive some quotations with information regarding models and prices together with details of terms and timings of delivery.

Figure 5.5

JUNGLEWORLD LTD
Casterford
CF12 7TJ

VAT Reg No 640 62351

Tel 01778 353357
Fax 01778 333428

11 May 2001

The Sales Manager
Sweet Sensation Ltd
Westgate Works
Madderford
MA8 2RP

Dear Madam

I would be grateful if you could send specification details of your 'SweetBox' range including available package sizes and customisation options. Please include relevant prices with the delivery period and any carriage costs.

I look forward to your reply.

Yours sincerely

DKerslake

Debbie Kerslake
(Director)

Registered office: JungleWorld, Casterford CF12 7TJ   Registered number: 53186223

Figure 5.6 *Letter of enquiry*

Key terms

A **letter of enquiry** is a letter to a supplier requesting information regarding specifications, prices and availability for a given product or product range.
A **quotation** is a statement of product details and price available at a given date or for a given length of time.

Sweet Sensation Ltd
Westgate Works
Madderford
MA8 2RP

VAT Reg No 322 699482

Tel 01421 863577
Fax 01421 886444

15 May 2001

Ms D Kerslake
JungleWorld
Casterford
CF12 7TJ

Dear Ms Kerslake

Thank you for your letter dated 11 May. Our SweetBox range features assorted fruit flavoured boiled sweets in 200g and 400g boxes. The boxes can be customised with your name and logo at no extra cost.

For orders in excess of 200 boxes, the prices are:

200g @ £1.25
400g @ £2.00

The delivery period is 21 days from the receipt of an order and carriage is free of charge.

Please note that this quotation is valid for 3 months from the date of this letter.

We look forward to receiving your order.

Yours sincerely

Adrian O'Dell

Adrian O'Dell
(Sales Manager)

Registered office: Sweet Sensation Ltd, Westgate Works, Madderf...
Registered number: 4517203

Figure 5.7 *Quotation*

Debbie decides to order 500 JungleBoxes at £2.00 each and issues a purchase order:

JUNGLEWORLD LTD
Casterford
CF12 7TJ

VAT Reg No 640 62351

Tel 01778 353357
Fax 01778 333428

21 May 2001

The Sales Manager
Sweet Sensation Ltd
Westgate Works
Madderford
MA8 2RP

Quantity	Catalogue No.	Description	Price £
500	SB1	400g SweetBox (inscription: JungleBox)	2.00 each

Delivery to:
JungleWorld office
Casterford
CF12 7TJ

Delivery to be received within 21 days from receipt of order. No charge for carriage.

Thank you.

DKerslake

Debbie Kerslake
(Director)

Registered office: JungleWorld, Casterford CF12 7TJ   Registered number: 53186223

Figure 5.8 *Purchase order*

The purchase order usually includes details of the products being ordered (often with a reference or catalogue number), the date and place of delivery and the relevant price. The seller will usually issue and send an acknowledgement which thanks the buyer for their order, confirms product availability and indicates the scheduled date of delivery. Not long before the goods are actually despatched, the seller may also send an advice note which tells the buyer that their order has been despatched and should be received after any period in transit.

Sweet Sensation Ltd
Westgate Works
Madderford
MA8 2RP

VAT Reg No 322 699482

Tel 01421 863577
Fax 01421 886444

24 May 2001

Ms D Kerslake
JungleWorld
Casterford
CF12 7TJ

Dear Ms Kerslake

Order No. 0154

Thank you for your order dated 21 May.

We can confirm that your order will be despatched on the terms agreed to your address as above.

Order details:

500 X 400g SweetBox (inscription: JungleWorld) Catalogue No. SB1 @ £2.00 each.

Yours sincerely

Adrian O'Dell
(Sales Manager)

Registered office: Sweet Sensation Ltd, Westgate Works, Madderford MA8 2RP
Registered number: 4517203

Figure 5.9 *Acknowledgement*

ASE STUDY

JungleWorld

A van has arrived with 25 cartons containing 20 boxes of sweets. The driver also wants a delivery note signed and leaves a copy for Debbie. Unfortunately one carton has been crushed. The van driver doubts whether it will matter.

Sweet Sensation Ltd
Westgate Works
Madderford
MA8 2RP

VAT Reg No 322 699482

Tel 01421 863577
Fax 01421 886444

11 June 2001

Ms D Kerslake
JungleWorld
Casterford
CF12 7TJ

Order No. 0154
Despatch details: 25 cartons by road.

Quantity	Catalogue	Desription
500	SB1	400g SweetBoxes Inscription: JungleBox

Delivery to:

JungleWorld
Casterford
CF12 7TJ

Aaron O'D.ll

Adrian O'Dell
(Sales Manager)

- -

Received: 25 cartons

Signed _

On behalf of _

Registered office: Sweet Sensation Ltd, Westgate Works, Madderford MA8 2RP
Registered number: 4517203

Figure 5.10 *Delivery note*

The delivery note states exact details of the products delivered and allows the buyer to check that the delivery corresponds with the original order. The delivery note will shortly be followed by an invoice. This is a key document which states the products that have been purchased, their price (plus any VAT) and the sum of money now owed.

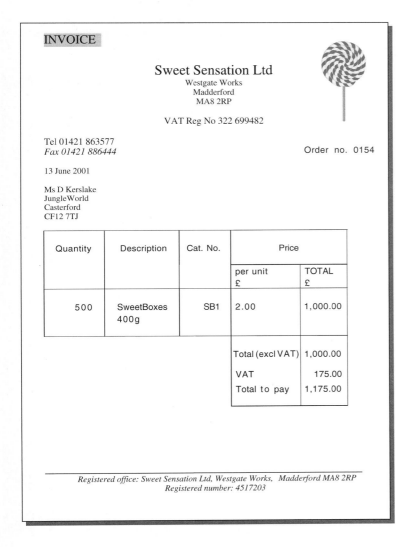

INVOICE

Sweet Sensation Ltd
Westgate Works
Madderford
MA8 2RP

VAT Reg No 322 699482

Tel 01421 863577
Fax 01421 886444

Order no. 0154

13 June 2001

Ms D Kerslake
JungleWorld
Casterford
CF12 7TJ

Quantity	Description	Cat. No.	Price	
			per unit £	TOTAL £
500	SweetBoxes 400g	SB1	2.00	1,000.00
			Total (excl VAT)	1,000.00
			VAT	175.00
			Total to pay	1,175.00

Registered office: Sweet Sensation Ltd, Westgate Works, Madderford MA8 2RP
Registered number: 4517203

Figure 5.11 *Invoice*

Key terms

A **delivery note** is a statement of goods being delivered and usually requires a signature to confirm receipt.
An **invoice** informs a buyer the products that they have received, the amount owing and the latest date for payment.

The seller will generally try to issue the invoice as soon as possible since this will generate cash flow and reduce the opportunity cost of resources tied up as debtors.

For regular or larger customers, the seller may send a statement of account which summarises for a given period the invoices outstanding as debits and any payments received (or credit notes, see page 16) as credits. The balance is the total amount due to be paid.

 **Cash flow, page 58**

 **Opportunity cost, page 6**

 **Debtors, page 31**

CASE STUDY

Sweet Sensation and JungleWorld

Rosa checks the boxes in the consignment from Sweet Sensation and finds that one box has been crushed, damaging the cartons inside. She phones the despatch office at Sweet Sensation and they agree to issue a credit note to cover the value of the damaged goods.

CREDIT NOTE	No. 00094

Sweet Sensation Ltd
Westgate Works
Madderford
MA8 2RP

VAT Reg No 322 699482

Tel 01421 863577
Fax 01421 886444

Date/tax point: 14 June 2001

Ms D Kerslake (Director)
JungleWorld
Casterford
CF12 7TJ

Quantity	Description	Cat. No.	Per unit £	Total £
20	SweetBox 400g	SB1	2.00	40.00

Total excluding VAT	40.00
VAT	7.00
Total credit	47.00

Reason for credit:

Carton containing 20 X SB1 damaged

(Purchase Order No. 0154; Invoice No. 04418)

Registered office: Sweet Sensation Ltd, Westgate Works, Madderford MA8 2RP
Registered number: 4517203

Figure 5.12 *Credit note*

JungleWorld now decides to settle the invoice for its consignment of goods from Sweet Sensation. A document called a remittance advice. is issued by the accounts department.

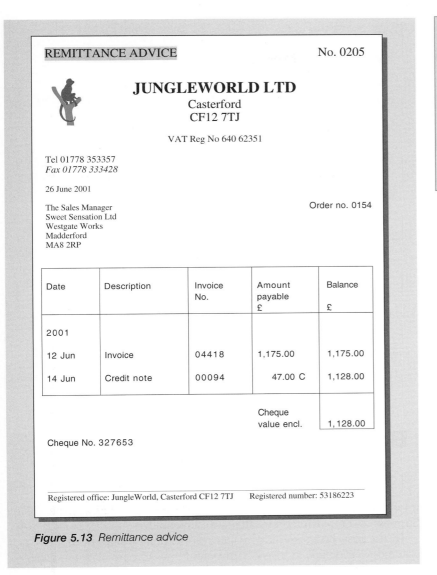

REMITTANCE ADVICE   No. 0205

JUNGLEWORLD LTD
Casterford
CF12 7TJ

VAT Reg No 640 62351

Tel 01778 353357
Fax 01778 333428

26 June 2001

The Sales Manager   Order no. 0154
Sweet Sensation Ltd
Westgate Works
Madderford
MA8 2RP

Date	Description	Invoice No.	Amount payable £	Balance £
2001				
12 Jun	Invoice	04418	1,175.00	1,175.00
14 Jun	Credit note	00094	47.00 C	1,128.00
			Cheque value encl.	1,128.00

Cheque No. 327653

Registered office: JungleWorld, Casterford CF12 7TJ   Registered number: 53186223

Figure 5.13 *Remittance advice*

The remittance advice states which invoice(s) the buyer is settling and indicates any credit items such as a payment already remitted. In smaller firms a cheque may be handwritten and enclosed with the remittance advice. Otherwise the computer system will generate the remittance advice and cheque together, the cheque being detachable and ready for payment into the bank.

Key term

The **bank clearing system** involves a paid-in cheque being sent to London for sorting by bank and relevant branch and being returned to the drawer's branch where it is 'cleared' and the appropriate amount of money transferred to the account of the payee.

ASE STUDY

Sweet Sensation

When Rosa receives the remittance advice from JungleWorld, her assistant takes the cheque and the company's 'paying in' book to the bank. He pays in the cheque by completing a paying-in slip and having the counterfoil stamped.

Once a paying-in slip is completed, the cheque enters the bank clearing system and will take three working days to appear as a credit in Sweet Sensation's bank account.

Receipt	Paying in request	firstBank plc
Sort code and account number		
	Branch where the account is held	Account in the name(s) of
Branch stamp	Branch sort code	
	Account number	Enter totals from overleaf
		Cash £
	Your signature	Postal orders £
Cash £		Cheques £
Postal Orders £		Total £
Cheques £		
Total paid in £	11006-1200 Please use only to pay into a firstBank plc account.	E credit

Figure 5.14 Paying-in slip

Book-keeping

We have looked at a range of financial documents that record the process of transactions in business. The next step is to see how the information they contain can be assembled to help in running the business and reporting on its affairs to stakeholders.

In the past, businesses kept paper records of all transactions and entered their details in heavy hard-bound books where all totals were calculated manually. Today the term 'book-keeping' remains but most firms use computer systems for their accounting procedures with a software package that may be 'off the shelf' or customised to meet their needs. However, the principles of book-keeping and accounting are unchanged.

Books of original entry

The initial recording of business transactions takes place in books of original or prime entry. These include:

- purchases day book where all credit purchases are recorded
- sales day book where all credit sales are recorded
- cash book.

Date	Details	Invoice	Folio	Net £	VAT £	Gross £
2001						
3 Apr	Laing & Ball Ltd	5330	SM35	132.00	23.10	155.10
7 Apr	D Margetts	6241	SM42	28.00	4.90	32.90
15 Apr	Rand Corporation	K1542	SM19	810.00	141.75	951.75
17 Apr	Beckwith Bros	7710	SM43	216.00	37.80	253.80
29 Apr	Trubshaw & Co	2634	SM50	58.00	10.15	68.15
30	Totals		TM94	1,244.00	217.70	1,461.70

Figure 5.15 *Purchases day book*

Date	Details	Invoice	Folio	Net £	VAT £	Gross £
2001						
4 Apr	Warren Bros	408	SB12	640.00	112.00	752.00
14 Apr	Pengelly & Co	409	SB41	206.00	36.05	242.05
20 Apr	Lavender's Ltd	410	SB7	320.00	56.00	376.00
22 Apr	Rowe & Sons	411	SB18	58.00	10.15	68.15
30 Apr	Totals		TR64	1,224.00	214.20	1,438.20

Figure 5.16 *Sales day book*

Date	Details	Cash £	Bank £	Date	Details	Cash £	Bank £
2001				2001			
1 May	Balance b/d	100.00	1,000.00	6 May	K Reeve	45.00	
3 May	N Edwards	70.00		13 May	Wages to S Gooding	110.00	
11 May	S Harvey & Co		285.00	20 May	Small's Ltd		130.00
18 May	P Mace-Butler	120.00		29 May	Diamond & Co	65.00	
25 May	Richards Ltd		180.00		Balance c/d	70.00	1,335.00
		290.00	1,465.00			290.00	1,465.00
1 Jun	Balance b/d	70.00	1,335.00				

Figure 5.17 *Cash book*

The purchases and sales day books are based on invoices received and issued by the business and therefore relate to credit transactions. The folio column carries an account reference which enables links to be made with other parts of the book-keeping system. The 'net' and 'gross' columns allow VAT inclusive and exclusive data to be kept. The day books are totalled at regular intervals, which could be daily, weekly or monthly.

The double entry principle

A business maintains a number of different accounts, each covering significant areas of income or expenditure. As each financial transaction occurs it can be understood and recorded from two points of view:
- the account that is 'receiving' value
- the account that is 'giving up' value.

This is the basis of double entry (or dual aspect) accounting. The traditional format for recording entries distinguishes:
- debits ('DR' – from debitors) on the left-hand side
- credits ('CR' – from creditors) on the right-hand side.

At first encounter this is a rather confusing idea. We tend to think simply of a debit as money taken away and a credit as money coming in. Double entry is best understood in terms of different accounts and therefore different viewpoints of the same transaction.

CASE STUDY

Chris Richardson is an all-terrain cycling enthusiast who makes 'new' bicycles from old parts. He has just bought ten frames on credit for £240.

In his Purchases account he makes a debit entry for £240 and then in his Creditors account he will record a credit entry for £240.

The double entry is:

Purchases account	debit £240
Creditors account	credit £240

One month later a cheque payment of £240 is made to the supplier of the frames. This time the double entry is:

Creditors account	debit £240
Bank account	credit £240

Figure 5.18 reCYCLES

In the first transaction, notice that in terms of purchases the business has received value while in terms of creditors the firm is 'giving up' value.

In the second transaction, notice that in terms of creditors the firm has 'received value' from the payment while in terms of the bank account the firm has 'given up' value.

The cash book

The cash book is part of the double entry system and records all cash and bank transactions. It generally uses a column format to include the folio reference and allow entries for cash and bank transactions.

In larger firms the cash book will be the responsibility of a cashier who will also control the petty cash.

Ledgers

Ledgers used to be heavy bound volumes that contained each of the company's key accounts. Although they are now mainly computerised, the term 'ledgers' has the same meaning. Typically a business might maintain the following ledgers:

- a purchases ledger recording all purchases and including specific supplier accounts
- a sales ledger recording all sales and including specific customer accounts
- a general ledger recording all other expenditure (and income) including salaries, wages, overhead expenses and the purchase of assets.

Once again entries are made in these ledgers on the double entry principle. An example should make the process clearer.

CASE STUDY

reCYCLES

The following financial tranactions occurred at **reCYCLES** over the month of April 2001:

1 April	Started the business with £5,000 in bank
1 April	Bought stock of components for £500 on credit
3 April	Purchased equipment for £1,750 by cheque
7 April	Paid £100 in wages to part-time assistant
17 April	Sold £150 worth of goods for cash
25 April	Paid £250 rent by cheque
29 April	Sold goods to the value of £450 on credit

The relevant ledger entries read as follows:

DR				CR		
Date	Item	£		Date	Item	£

Capital account

DR				CR		
1 April	Balance c/f	5,000		1 April	Cash	5,000
					Balance b/f	5,000

Purchases account

DR				CR		
1 April	Creditors	500		1 April	Balance c/f	500
	Balance b/f	500				

Creditors account

DR				CR		
1 April	Balance c/f	500		1 April	Purchases	500
					Balance b/f	500

Equipment account

DR				CR		
3 April	Cash	1,750		3 April	Balance c/f	1,750
	Balance b/f	1,750				

Wages account

DR				CR		
7 April	Cash	100		7 April	Balance c/f	100
	Balance b/f	100				

Sales account

DR				CR		
17 April	Balance c/f	600		17 April	Cash	150
				29 April	Debtors	450
						600

Rentals account

DR				CR		
25 April	Cash	250		25 April	Balance c/f	250
	Balance b/f	250				

Debtors account

DR				CR		
29 April	Sales	450		29 April	Balance c/f	450
	Balance	450				

Cashbook

Dr					Cr				
Date	Item	Folio	Cash	Bank	Date	Item	Folio	Cash	Bank
1 Apr	Capital	X27		5,000					
17 Apr	Sales	S42	150		3 Apr	Purchases	P66		1,750
					7 Apr	Wages	C54	100	
					25 Apr	Rent	Y34		250
						Balance c/f		50	3,000
			150	5,000				150	5,000
	Balance b/f		50	3,000					

Figure 5.19 Ledger entries

These ledgers when taken together form a meaningful picture of the financial transactions that make up a working business.

Trial balance

This is not a double entry account but a checking device which involves totalling the ledger entries. If they are correct, then the two columns of debits and credits should balance since they are simply different ways of looking at the same transactions.

ⒸASE STUDY

reCYCLES

Chris Richardson is now preparing his first trial balance for the month of April:

Trial balance as at 30 April 2001

	DR	CR
Capital		5,000
Purchases	500	
Equipment	1,750	
Wages	100	
Sales		600
Rentals	250	
Debtors	450	
Creditors		500
Cash book	50	
Bank	3,000	
	6,100	6,100

Figure 5.20 *Trial balance*

At the end of an accounting period, the ledgers provide the financial information for construction of the balance sheet and profit and loss account. The accounting period varies between organisations but could be a month, a quarter, a half year or a full year.

 Profit and loss account, page 32

The balance sheet

What is the balance sheet? Imagine the chief executive of a business suddenly shouting 'Stop!' For a moment, all activity in the firm is frozen and a count is made to identify everything of value being used by the firm at that precise time. A list of resources in use and their value is exactly matched by another list of how the resources were obtained or – put another way – who would have to be paid if they were all sold. Taken together these two lists form a balance sheet.

It is easy to see why the total value of the two lists is the same. One list itemises everything of value in the business. The other states who provided the same resources. It is therefore no coincidence that the two lists show an equal total value: they are just two different ways of looking at the same resources.

Want to know more?

All non-trading data for the balance sheet is found in the General Ledger including changes in shareholders' or owners' capital, borrowings and fixed assets. Trading data is recorded in the Purchases and Sales Ledgers. The current stock level and the value of debtors and creditors can be extracted from these ledgers while the values of cash in hand and cash at the bank are found in the Cash Book.

CASE STUDY

Character Cards

Laura Metcalf and Donna Choi decided to set up in business and cater for a niche market in greetings cards not served by the major manufacturers. In 2001 the enterprise was launched in Donna's house with £3,000 savings and a £1,500 bank loan. At the start of the first year's trading, most of this money had been spent on a computer plus software, equipment such as tables and lighting and stocks of card and paper.

Balance sheet as at 1 April 2001

Sources of Funds	£	Uses of Funds	£
Bank loan	1,500	Computer & software	2,000
Owners' funds	3,000	Equipment	500
		Stocks	1,500
		Cash	500
	4,500		4,500

Figure 5.22 *Balance sheet for Character Cards (April)*

Figure 5.21 Character Cards

Balance sheets are always given an exact date since they relate to a particular moment in time. That is why they are sometimes called a 'snapshot' of the business.

How does a balance sheet reflect a change in the resources used by a firm? Normally, balance sheets are only drawn up at yearly or half yearly intervals. But in theory there is nothing to prevent a new balance sheet being constructed every day.

Suppose that after a month Character Cards decides to spend £250 in cash on some display units. How would this affect the balance sheet?

CASE STUDY

Balance sheet as at 1 May 2001

Sources of Funds	£	Uses of Funds	£
Bank loan	1,500	Computer & software	2,000
Owners' funds	3,000	Equipment	750
		Stocks	1,500
		Cash	250
	4,500		4,500

Figure 5.23 *Balance sheet for Character Cards (May)*

Notice that this is a change only in the Use of Funds. It is clear that cash will fall back to £250. The equipment value will rise to £750. Total Uses of Funds will remain at £4,500. No change is needed to the Sources of Funds since we are only juggling with resources already in the business.

Now what would happen if £1,000 worth of stock is sold over the next month for £2,000? The same logic is followed.

CASE STUDY

Balance sheet as at 1 June 2001

Sources of Funds	£	Uses of Funds	£
Bank loan	1,500	Computer & software	2,000
Owners' funds	3,000	Equipment	750
Add: net profit	1,000	Stocks	500
		Cash	2,250
	5,500		5,500

Figure 5.24 *Balance sheet for Character Cards (June)*

First we reduce stock to £500. Then we can increase cash to £2,250. But now there is a problem. The source of funds adds up to £4,500 and the uses of funds totals £5,500. The answer lies in the profit that has been made: £1,000. That money is now in the business bank account but it has added £1,000 to the owners' funds. The left-hand side now balances at £5,500.

It is unlikely that this money will remain as cash for long. Over the following month Laura and Donna use £500 to pay for more stock, £1,000 to buy a secondhand van and £500 to cut the bank loan. These changes need taking in stages:

(a) Stock value rises back to £1,000 and cash falls to £1,750.

(b) The value of the van appears as vehicles and cash falls further to £750.

(c) Bank loans fall to £1,000 and cash is cut again to £250.

(a) Sources of Funds		Uses of Funds	
	£		£
Bank loan	1,500	Computer etc.	2,000
		Equipment	750
Owners' funds	4,000	Stocks	1,000
		Cash	1,750
	5,500		5,500

Figure 5.25 *Balance sheet after (a) during July 2001*

(b) Sources of Funds		Uses of Funds	
	£		£
Bank loan	1,500	Computer etc.	2,000
Owners' funds	4,000	Vehicles	1,000
		Equipment	750
		Stocks	1,000
		Cash	750
	5,500		5,500

Figure 5.26 *Balance sheet after (b) during July 2001*

(c) Sources of Funds		Uses of Funds	
	£		£
Bank loan	1,000	Computer etc.	2,000
		Vehicles	1,000
Owners' funds	4,000	Equipment	750
		Stocks	1,000
		Cash	250
	5,000		5,000

Figure 5.27 *Balance sheet after (c) during July 2001*

You will notice that when any value changes on the balance sheet, another value changes too. This is again the principle of double entry. It exists because every time a change takes place in the source or use of funds in a business, it must involve:

- a change from one use to another, *or*
- a change from one source to another, *or*
- change in a source and a use.

The T-form balance sheet

The format for the balance sheet used so far is called the T-form because its layout is based on the shape of a capital 'T'. The left-hand side answers the question 'Where did the money come from?' and the right-hand side answers the corresponding question 'Where is the money now?' In practice the traditional T-form balance sheet has been replaced by a modern vertical format. However, this is much easier to follow once the T-form has been properly understood.

All the uses of funds represent assets. The sources of funds are either liabilities – owed to others – or belong to the firm's owners – the sole proprietor, the partners or the shareholders.

Individual items on the balance sheet are arranged according to a pattern:

Sources of Funds	Uses of Funds
Owners'/shareholders' funds	Fixed assets
Long-term liabilities	
Current liabilities	Current assets

Figure 5.28 The T-form pattern

In general, items that will stay in the firm longest come first. So owners' or shareholders' funds are followed by loans that are repayable after more than 12 months – the long-term liabilities. The current liabilities – money that must be paid back in less than 12 months – come last. In the same way, fixed assets are items that usually stay in the business for years whereas current assets 'circulate' as the firm trades. We now have a picture of the resources in a firm as expressed on the balance sheet.

**CTIVITY**

Lightning Ltd

Run by Darren Beesley and Dawn Newman, this Coventry-based enterprise was launched in 2000 to sell and service rollerskates and rollerblades. It also sells a wide range of accessories from its cramped premises. Dawn is not familiar with accounting methods and on 31 March 2001 produces a rather jumbled list of information from which a balance sheet must be constructed:

	£
Vehicle	1,500
Debtors	2,500
Business rates	750
Creditors	6,500
Cash	3,250
Bank loan	8,500
Stock	11,750

Wages (for year)	21,250
Equipment	6,000
Rent (per month)	250
Owners' capital	10,000

Figure 5.29 *Lightning Ltd*

Tasks

1 Produce a simple T-form balance sheet for Lightning Ltd as at 31 March 2001.
2 Which items of information on Dawn's list did you *not* use? Why not?

Using vertical format

Nowadays firms use a vertical format to present their balance sheet in columns. This looks very different from the T-form but it is actually just a rearrangement of the same building blocks.

The vertical format is constructed around the following system:

> ### all assets in the business
> *less*
> ### all borrowing by the business
> *equals*
> ### all shareholders' funds

Figure 5.30 *Simple vertical format*

Think about this carefully. Take the value of everything a business owns, then strip out every amount that it owes. Now the value that is left must belong to the owners or shareholders. Once again we have a 'balance'.

We can now apply an expanded version of this format to a major public company: Cadbury-Schweppes plc.

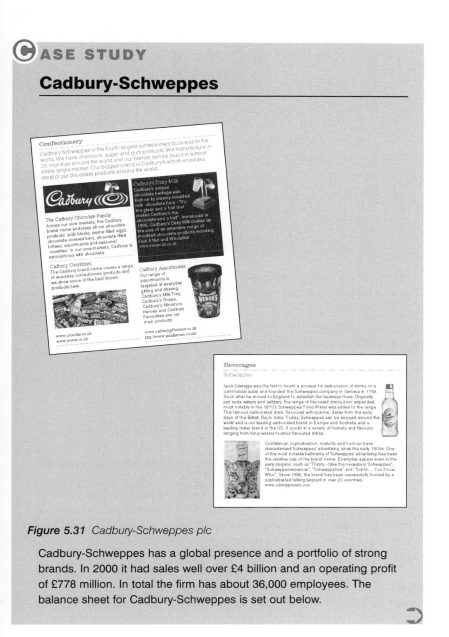

CASE STUDY

Cadbury-Schweppes

Figure 5.31 Cadbury-Schweppes plc

Cadbury-Schweppes has a global presence and a portfolio of strong brands. In 2000 it had sales well over £4 billion and an operating profit of £778 million. In total the firm has about 36,000 employees. The balance sheet for Cadbury-Schweppes is set out below.

	£m	£m
Fixed Assets		
Tangible assets	1,106	
Intangible assets	3,163	
Investments	456	4,725
Current Assets		
Stocks	458	
Debtors	923	
Cash	174	
Other	334	
	1,889	
Current Liabilities		
Creditors	(2,937)	
Net Current Assets		(1,048)
Total Assets less Current Liabilities		3,677
Long-term Liabilities		
Creditors	(489)	
Provisions	(261)	(750)
		2,927
Shareholders' Funds		
Share capital	255	
Share premium account	991	
Revaluation & other reserves	152	
Profit & Loss account	1,234	2,632
Minority interests		295
		2,927

Figure 5.32 *Cadbury-Schweppes plc: Balance Sheet as at 31 December 2000*

It is important to be clear about the terms and structure used in the vertical format. Two columns are often used for adding and subtracting. This is useful since it allows sub-totals in the first column and grand totals in the second column.

Fixed Assets is straightforward and exactly as used in T-form.

Current Assets and *Current Liabilities* are also familiar but this time current liabilities are subtracted from current assets to give *Net Current Assets* (i.e. net of current liabilities), which is also often called working capital.

This value is then added to *Fixed Assets* to give *Total Assets less Current Liabilities* – a clumsy term that speaks for itself!

Long-term Liabilities are now stripped out to give a final total called *Net Assets*. This is really total assets net of all liabilities to external parties. It balances – as you might expect – with total *Shareholders' Funds* or *Capital Employed*. So the vertical format balances on the resources truly owned by the business itself. Notice that this will be a lower value than the balancing figure using T-form. This is because T-form balances on total resources in the business including those funded by borrowing.

The balance sheet in close-up

'Fixed assets' are all those items of value in the firm that help to generate income but are not 'passing through' the business. 'Tangible assets' meaning 'touchable' fixed assets include all land, buildings, plant and equipment. Some firms also quote a value for intangible fixed assets. This often refers to brands or patents that have been given a money value. For example, Cadbury-Schweppes, who owns brands such as Canada Dry and Sunkist soft drinks, Roses chocolates and Trebor confectionery, values its brands at £2,354 million. There may also be an entry for 'Investments' made by the company outside the operations of its own business. These will yield an income which appears in the profit and loss account.

'Current Assets' are those items of value in the firm that are passing through the business in the course of its operations. 'Stocks' includes raw materials, work-in-progress and finished goods.

Firms selling services may have stocks of consumables, such as stationery, and can have work-in-progress where services to customers are not complete. Retailers obviously have stocks of unsold goods.

'Debtors' includes all amounts of money that are owed to the firm. This usually means customers who have not yet settled their bills. 'Cash' includes money in the firm's bank accounts plus any petty cash in the tills or safe.

'Current Liabilities' refers to all amounts of money that must be paid by the business to outsiders over the next 12 months. The main item is usually trade creditors which includes all amounts owed to suppliers. Bank overdrafts and short-term loans also count as current liabilities.

'Long-term Liabilities' consists of all loans repayable in more than 12 months' time. This is an important figure when calculating ROCE (Return on Capital Employed).

'Shareholders' Funds' or equity is the money in the business that belongs to the owners or shareholders. The shares in a company can only be issued up to a value that is specified in the Memorandum of Association.

When shares are issued and sold there may be a time lapse between the firm requiring part and full payment. The money that has been raised is termed 'called up share capital'.

In practice, the largest part of the Shareholders' Funds is usually in the form of Reserves. This is a rather confusing term and it does not mean money 'put on one side' or held in reserve. Instead it primarily refers to past profits that belong to the shareholders but are invested in the assets of the business.

> **Key term**
>
> **Work-in-progress** includes all goods that are at some stage in the process of transformation into finished products.

 ROCE, pages 37–38

> **Key term**
>
> The **Memorandum of Association** is a legal document drawn up by a company when it begins trading. It specifies the internal rules for the company, including the number of shares that can be issued.

We can look at the main types of reserve. At issue, shares are given a 'nominal value' such as 50p or £1. Often the actual price charged is higher than the nominal value and the difference appears as the 'Share Premium Account'. The Revaluation Reserve arises when fixed assets – particularly land and buildings – increase in value. The firm will have some fixed assets revalued at regular intervals. Plant and equipment *depreciate*: that is, they fall in value. The Revaluation Reserve is generated by those assets that *appreciate* in value. Finally, the Profit & Loss Account refers to what is often the largest item in the Reserves and represents accumulated retained profits.

I Has a profit been made?

Every business needs to know: to what extent have we been successful (or unsuccessful) in adding value to resources and generating a profit? The profit and loss account is designed to answer this vital question. Put simply, it is a statement of turnover or sales revenue followed by a listing of the costs incurred to achieve those sales. The difference is profit.

Constructing the profit and loss account is quite straightforward. Gross profit is calculated by taking the value of sales and subtracting the cost of sales – the value of purchases and the cost of wages. Net profit is then found by subtracting all the overhead expenses (such as salaries, rents and marketing costs) from the gross profit.

The document ends with an indication of how any profit was used or 'appropriated'. In practice, profit has several different values because it has several distinct definitions. As successive types of cost are subtracted, we arrive at a series of different sub-totals for profit.

C ASE STUDY

Internet Investments plc

	£m
Sales revenue/turnover	100
Less Cost of sales	40
= Gross profit	60
Less Overhead costs	20
= Net or Operating profit	40

Less Exceptional items	5
= Profit before interest	35
Less Interest expense	5
= Profit before tax	30
Less Taxation expense	8
= Profit after tax	22
Less Dividends	10
= Retained profit	12

Figure 5.33

We will follow through this correct pattern with the accounts of Cadbury-Schweppes plc.

CASE STUDY

Cadbury-Schweppes plc

	2000
	£m
Turnover	4,575
Cost of sales	2,160
	2,415

Figure 5.34 Profit and Loss Account for year ending 31 December 2000 (extract)

This is the first stage in the profit and loss and tells us how much profit was made on sales without allowing for overhead costs.

ACTIVITY

New Look Plc

	1999	2000
	£m	£m
Turnover	418	367
Cost of sales	327	286
	91	81

Figure 5.35 Profit and Loss Account for years ending 25 March 1999/2000

Tasks

1 What was the company's gross profit and gross profit margin in 2000?
2 Make comparisons with 1999.
3 Try researching the relevant data for 2001 (or later years).

value of sales

less

cost of sales

equals

gross profit

('includes no allowance for overheads')

Figure 5.36 Calculating gross profit

Cost of sales is the direct cost of 'what-has-been-sold'. In a manufacturing firm it will include direct labour and direct materials. For a retailer, the calculation would be based on changes in the value of stock.

CASE STUDY

Ace Trading Ltd

	£k	£k
Sales		100
Opening stock	15	
plus Purchases	60	
= Available stock	75	
Less Closing stock	(10)	
= Cost of goods sold		65
Gross profit		35

Figure 5.37

After gross profit we subtract the relevant overhead costs:

	£m
Gross profit	2,415
Selling expenses	(1,272)
Adminstrative expenses	(430)
Operating profit (or net profit)	713*

*excluding associate companies

Figure 5.38 Cadbury-Schweppes plc: Simplified extract from Profit and Loss Account for year ending 31 January 2000

Selling expenses may also be called 'distribution costs' and generally include the costs of marketing. Administrative expenses is a 'catch all' term and includes all other overheads such as management salaries, rent and insurance. Some firms will also quote R & D (Research and Development) expenses. Operating profit is found when these deductions have been made. It may also be called trading profit and is often called net profit by smaller companies.

What happens to profit?

CASE STUDY

Cadbury-Schweppes plc

	£
Operating profit	778[1]
Exceptional items	27
Profit before interest and tax	805
Net interest payable	(49)
Profit before tax	756
Tax on profit	(224)
Profit after tax	532
Dividends	(209)
Retained profit[2]	287

[1]including profit from associated companies
[2]after deducting share of profits for minority interests (£36m)

Figure 5.39 *Extract from profit and loss account for year ended 31 December 2000 (Source: Cadbury-Schweppes plc Annual Report and Accounts 2000)*

The next stage of the profit and loss account includes any exceptional items. These financial impacts are given special treatment because of their size or infrequency. Typically they include the costs or proceeds of closing down certain operations (e.g. a chain of loss-making shops) or an unexpected bad debt. Once allowance has been made for exceptional items, 'Profit before interest and tax' remains.

'Net interest payable' includes interest on Cadbury-Schweppes's borrowing less the interest received on the company's own bank and investment accounts.

'Profit before tax' is the sub-total liable to corporation tax. This is generally charged at around 30 per cent for large companies but at a reduced rate for small companies with profits of less than £250,000. A complex system of tax allowances means that the actual percentage rates paid will vary.

'Profit after tax' may be reduced further by payments to 'minority interests'. This simply means that the firm owns less than 100 per cent of the shares in some subsidiary companies and the 'outside' shareholders

Key term

Bad debts are debts that are unlikely to be settled. They can sometimes be sold at a discount to a debt collection agency.

Key term

Retained profit is the profit remaining after dividends have been paid, that is re-invested in the company.

must be given their share of those companies' profits. Otherwise profit after tax is available for use as the directors decide. In 2000 Cadbury-Schweppes distributed as dividends about 42 per cent of its available profit after tax. The equivalent proportion at Tesco was 45 per cent. For Marks & Spencer – who suffered a sharp fall in profits – the figure was 100 per cent, meaning that retained profit was virtually zero. In theory at least, there is nothing to stop shareholders instructing the directors to distribute more or less profit in the form of dividends. In reality the directors set the dividend level but are careful to satisfy shareholders, especially the fund managers of such institutions as insurance companies and pension funds.

ACTIVITY

Cadbury-Schweppes plc

	2000 £	1999 £
Turnover	4,575	4,301
Cost of sales	(2,160)	(2,136)
Gross profit	2,415	2,165
Overhead expenses	(1,702)	(1,531)
Operating profit	713	634
Other profits/(losses)[1]	92	385
Profit before interest	805	1,019
Interest payable	(49)	(61)
Profit before tax	756	958
Tax payable	(224)	(215)
Profit after tax	532	743
Dividends	(209)	(202)
Retained profit[2]	287	440

[1]includes share of profit from associate companies and sales of subsidiaries and investments

[2]after payments to minority interests (£36m in 2000 and £101m in 1999)

Figure 5.40 Profit and Loss Account for financial years ending 1999 and 2000

Task

Assess changes in the company's performance between 1999 and 2000.

Key ratios

Most of a firm's stakeholder groups are interested in business performance. There is no perfect way of answering the question 'Is the firm efficient?' but the published accounts provide many vital clues. Directors and senior managers will monitor financial results as they become available but the obligation to publish accounts means that all stakeholders can make their own assessments. For large public companies there is also a constant stream of analysis supporting City opinion.

What is efficiency? What financial results would represent a good performance? Every business organisation is using scarce resources that carry an opportunity cost. In other words, the assets controlled by a firm have alternative uses that would also add value. The directors' task is to use their resources in such a way that the shareholders have no reason to transfer their investment elsewhere. In fact, directors normally aim for the reverse effect: to be so successful that new resources are attracted into an expanding business.

We should not forget that the business environment is usually competitive. If management falters in its performance, there are competitors waiting to seize the firm's market share. And without a recovery in the longer run, a failing company is likely to be taken over.

Measuring efficiency

PizzaExpress

Founded in 1965, PizzaExpress is a chain of over 250 restaurants in Britain and Ireland with a further 25 outlets in other countries. The brand is taking an increasing share of the mid-price eating-out market with sales up by 238 per cent over the past four years.

2000	£m
Sales	150
Operating profit	32
Capital employed	89

Thorntons plc

Although Thorntons is a public company, it is still a business with a strong family influence. It produces chocolate and confectionery targeted at the luxury end of the market. There are over 400 company-owned shops in Britain and Ireland plus about 125 franchised outlets. Recently the expansion of Thorntons has run into some difficulties.

2000	£m
Sales	153
Operating profit	10.5
Capital employed	96

The most widely used measure of performance in checking that resources work efficiently is Return on Capital Employed (ROCE). This expresses the relationship between profit and capital employed as a percentage. More precisely, it is defined as follows.

Key term

City opinion refers to the views of investors, analysts and journalists based in the City of London where the Stock Exchange and many financial institutions are based.

 Stakeholders, page 50

 Opportunity cost, page 6

Figure 5.41

Figure 5.42

$$\text{ROCE} = \frac{\text{Operating (or net) profit}}{\text{Shareholders' funds} + \text{Long-term liabilities}}$$

Another important indicator of performance is the firm's profit margin. This represents the proportion of sales that is profit. It is useful to monitor the gross profit margin but the key value for analysis is the net or operating margin:

$$\text{Profit margin} = \frac{\text{Operating (or net) profit}}{\text{Turnover (sales)}}$$

Table 5.4 *ROCE and profit margin*

PizzaExpress 2000	%	Thorntons 2000	%
ROCE	36.0	ROCE	10.9
Profit margin	21.3	Profit margin	6.9

PizzaExpress looks as if it is a very successful company. Certainly it is expanding and attracting interest as a leader in the market segment. By contrast, Thorntons had a year of poor results. A steep rise in fixed costs and failures in marketing combined to drive down operating profits. The firm has decided to work on improving sales growth and net margins.

 **CTIVITY**

Tesco

In 2000 Tesco made a profit of £934 million on sales of £18,546 million. The value of its capital employed was £5,624 million.

Tasks

1 Calculate the ROCE and profit margin for Tesco.
2 Contrast the results with values for PizzaExpress and Thorntons.

However, to get a more accurate picture of a company's performance, we need to consider key data over a period of time – say, five years. This allows trends to be spotted and avoids the risk of being misled by an exceptionally good or bad year.

We can now look more carefully at a firm's performance. Relative to the value of its assets, is the business 'turning over' or selling its product quickly – or slowly? Every business enterprise experiences periods of fast and slow trade. But every firm has a typical 'speed' of turnover when taking into account its size, as measured by asset value. Usually, rapid turnover is linked with smaller margins while high margins are often earned on a slow turnover. For example, a supermarket chain such as Tesco has a low profit margin but a continual rapid turnover. By contrast, a jeweller in London's Bond Street would have a fairly slow turnover but a high margin of profit. The speed of turnover is measured by the asset turnover ratio:

$$\text{Asset turnover ratio} = \frac{\text{Turnover}}{\text{Capital employed}}$$

measured as a 'number of times'.

Firms always aim to make their assets work as hard as possible and therefore want asset turnover to be higher rather than lower. However, there is often a loosely connected trade-off between asset turnover and profit margin. Notice that asset turnover can normally be boosted by cutting margins. This may or may not increase overall profitability. Much depends on the market and the market segments in which the firm is positioned.

PizzaExpress
2000

Turnover	£150m
Capital employed	£89m
Asset turnover ratio	1.69 times

Thorntons
2000

Turnover	£153m
Capital employed	£96m
Asset turnover ratio	1.59 times

There is now an important relationship to notice:

$$\text{Profit margin} \times \text{asset turnover} = \text{ROCE}$$

i.e. $\dfrac{\text{Operating profit}}{\text{Sales}} \times \dfrac{\text{Sales}}{\text{Capital employed}} = \dfrac{\text{Operating profit}}{\text{Capital employed}}$

Performance as measured by ROCE has two roots. Profit margin could be explored in more detail by investigating the profit and loss account. For example, what was the firm's gross margin? Similarly, asset turnover could be explored further by analysis of the balance sheet. What was the ratio between operating profit and fixed assets? A range of interesting investigations is possible.

Is the stock shifting?

Stock in any form represents a use of resources that carries an opportunity cost. To improve efficiency, a firm needs to ensure that stock is 'turned over' and sold as quickly as possible. This process is measured using the stock turnover ratio:

$$\text{Stock turnover ratio} = \frac{\text{Stock}}{\text{Turnover}} \times 100$$

Alternatively the simple (non-percentage) ratio can be multiplied by 12 to give the stockholding period in months. This value answers the question: 'How many months' sales are represented by the level of stock?'

CASE STUDY

	PizzaExpress 2000	Thorntons 2000
Stock	£7.1m	£17.0m
Turnover	£150m	£153m
Stock turnover ratio	4.7%	11.1%
Stockholding period	0.57 months	1.3 months

A low stock turnover ratio suggests less working capital trapped in stocks as the cost of stockholding is spread over more sales. On the other hand if the ratio gets too low, the customers may find products unavailable and the firm may be losing the discounts from bulk purchasing.

The same kind of balancing problem applies to debtors. Almost all firms have debtors since there are generally customers who do not pay bills immediately. The trade debtors/turnover ratio is calculated as:

$$\frac{\text{Trade debtors}}{\text{Turnover}} \times 100$$

Often, a simple debtors/turnover ratio using the value quoted for 'debtors' on the balance sheet is an acceptable approximation. However, trade debtors (i.e. customers owing money) is the proper measure and this can be very different from 'debtors' as an overall total. The debt collection period is often calculated in months with the formula:

$$\text{Debtors/turnover ratio} \times 12$$

CASE STUDY

	PizzaExpress 2000	Thorntons 2000
Trade debtors	£0.7m	£9.1m
Turnover	£150m	£153m
Debtors/sales ratio	0.47%	5.9%
Debt collection period	0.06 months	0.71 months

A short debt collection period is the ideal as, again, less resources are tied up in working capital. But equally, most firms offer competitive credit terms to tempt customers and this may be an important part of their marketing mix. The very low ratio at PizzaExpress is not as impressive as it appears since most of their sales are meals paid for in cash at time of purchase.

CTIVITY

Invensys plc

Invensys plc is a global company engaged in manufacturing and software design for the automotive and controls industries.

2000	£m
Stock	1,058
Trade debtors	1,338
Sales	7,350

J Sainsbury plc

A UK-based retailer of foods and household materials.

2000	£m
Stock	986
Trade debtors	54
Sales	17,414

Tasks

1 Calculate the stock turnover ratios and debt collection periods for Invensys and Sainsbury's.
2 Why do you think the results are so different for these two firms?

I Measuring solvency

Every business must have access to sufficient cash for the settlement of debts and the purchase of necessary materials and resources. Access to cash does not depend only on having money in a bank account. All non-cash assets with a market value can be turned into cash given sufficient time. The crucial question is how quickly and how practicably can an asset be made liquid – or turned into cash? Usually it would be very slow and impracticable to sell fixed assets. It follows that the main source of liquidity is the current assets.

In assessing liquidity, accountants do not only look at cash on the balance sheet but also analyse the relationship between current assets and current liabilities. Current assets include cash and items that could be turned into cash relatively easily. Current liabilities include some key 'threats' to cash in the form of indebtedness. The difference between current assets and current liabilities is called working capital. While fixed capital includes the long-term assets such as a factory or an office block, working capital refers to the resources that circulate through the firm in the process of its trading activity. It follows, therefore, that the relationship between current assets and current liabilities is very important. This relationship is called the current ratio:

Key term

Solvency exists when the value of assets held by a business (or an individual) is greater than total debt.

Key term

Liquidity means the ability to raise cash in the short term.

$$\text{Current ratio} = \frac{\text{Current assets}}{\text{Current liabilities}}$$

Often current assets are greater than current liabilities by a factor of between 0.5 and 1.5. More significant than the exact figure is the trend from one accounting period to another. Every industry and firm has its own safe norms. What matters is any striking movement away from the usual ratio.

In practice, accountants also use a more severe test of liquidity called the Acid Test ratio. This is calculated in exactly the same way as the current ratio but with the value of stocks stripped out of current assets:

$$\text{Acid Test ratio} = \frac{\text{Current assets} - \text{Stock}}{\text{Current liabilities}}$$

In this ratio stock is excluded since it is less liquid and often its true market value is uncertain. Again, there is no one perfect value although a little under 1.0 is a safe average. However, values vary quite widely by industry and it is abnormal shifts away from the firm's norm that are more significant.

CASE STUDY

Uniq (formery Unigate)

Uniq plc is a large European food and distribution company.

	£m
Current assets	
Stock	197
Debtors	323
Cash	81
	601
Current liabilities	636
Current ratio	= 601 / 636 = 0.94
Acid Test ratio	= (601 – 197) / 636 = 0.64

Source: Annual Report and Accounts 2000

Figure 5.43 *Extract from Uniq plc accounts*

ACTIVITY

AstraZeneca is a global pharmaceutical company specialising in the development and sale of prescription medicines.

Figure 5.44 *AstraZeneca*

	£m	£m
Current Assets		
Stock	2,105	
Debtors	3,960	
Investments	3,429	
Cash	1,021	10,515
Current Liabilities		
Borrowings	214	
Other	6,683	6,897

Figure 5.45 *Extract from balance sheet as at 31 December 2000*

Tasks

1 Calculate (a) the current ratio; (b) the Acid Test ratio.
2 Uniq's liquidity ratios in 1999 were:
   Current ratio   = 1.34
   Acid Test ratio = 1.05
   Comment briefly on the data for 2000.

| The shareholder perspective

How can performance be assessed? We have already explored a range of ratios that indicate different aspects of a firm's performance. Among these Return on Capital Employed (ROCE) is probably the most useful overall measure. However, there are some other indicators that are especially useful to shareholders when making judgements.

 ROCE, pages 37–38

   A share in a company is exactly that: the ownership of a fraction of the company. Shares in companies are bought by investors for two main reasons:
   • the expectation that future profits will permit the payment of dividends
   • the expectation that the value of the shares will increase making possible their later sale at a profit.

For a company's shares to attract investors it is essential that they can be readily bought and sold. This liquidity is provided by the London Stock Exchange (and other stock markets abroad) where 'second hand' (i.e. post-issue) shares can be bought and sold at the market price.

 Liquidity, page 41

   Say a new Internet enterprise is launched with the sale of one million shares at £1 each. Even on the first day of trading in those shares it is likely that their value will change. Perhaps a newspaper article suggests that the company will win new customers or a major investor begins buying up the shares in the hope of a future gain. Almost at once the value of the company might rise by say 5 per cent. This means that one share or one millionth of the company is now worth £1.05.

If the company's progress matches early signs of success, then over time the share price may rise much further and more shares may be issued at higher prices than the original £1.00.

Of course the reverse trend might emerge. Every business is subject to competitive market forces and an uncertain external environment. Investors may find that their company is losing ground and its share price falling. In extreme cases the firm may enter liquidation and its shares become worthless.

CASE STUDY

Next plc

Suffering from a sharp rise in interest rates and hit hard by a deep recession in the housing market, Next shares had slumped to only 15p by the end of 1990. Yet the shares were destined to be a star performer of the 1990s. Costs were cut and the Next brand recovered its sparkle. A long recovery gathered momentum and by the summer of 1996 the shares had reached 851p in value. Although sales growth faltered and profit dipped in 1998, the company returned more strong results in 1999–2000 and the share price was standing at 921p in spring 2001.

Marks & Spencer plc

M&S was always regarded as one of the safest shares that an investor could hold. Through the 1990s the company expanded in the UK and overseas as its share price rose to 511p. Then in 1998 the success story faltered. The autumn range was not well received and trade did not recover in 1999. Profits warnings followed and soon it was clear that a giant was in trouble. As annual profits crashed from £1.1 billion to less than £500 million, the share price dropped to a low of 178p in late 2000.

When a company's shares increase (or decrease) in value, it follows that its market valuation increases (or decreases) by the same proportion. For example, if a firm has issued one million shares and they rise in value from 300p to 350p, then its market valuation or market capitalisation also rises from £3.0m to £3.5m. If another firm were to launch a takeover bid, it might have to offer more than 350p per share in order to persuade enough shareholders to sell.

So how far is the price of a share an indicator of the company's performance? It often makes a rough-and-ready guide. In the case of Marks & Spencer a more than 50 per cent fall in profits provoked a more than 50 per cent fall in the share price. But share prices are very volatile. Sharp rises and falls can be triggered by rumour alone while a share can climb dramatically in value before the company has even begun any significant trading.

(A)CTIVITY

Table 5.6 *Monsoon and Next*

Monsoon	Next
Profit for the financial year = £15.3m	Profit for the financial year = £157.6m
Dividends = £8.0m	Dividends = £73.7m
Number of ordinary shares = 17.8m	Number of ordinary shares = 336.6m
Share price at 2000 reporting date = 89p	Share price at 2000 reporting date = 870p

Tasks

1 Calculate for each company:
  a) dividends per share
  b) dividend yield
  c) earnings per share
  d) price/earnings ratio.
Comment briefly on your findings.
2 Why do you think investors might choose to keep their shares despite a company's disappointing performance?

Financial information and stakeholders

The term 'private enterprise' refers to any business that is not owned or run by central or local government. Generally a private sector firm is free to run its affairs in any way that its owners choose. A sole trader or a partnership is under no obligation to disclose information to anyone except details of tax liabilities to the Inland Revenue.

But a company does have public obligations. The privilege of limited liability carries a responsibility to disclose basic financial information. This is only reasonable since no more than the value of the assets is available to repay creditors.

Organisations within the public sector also have a duty to provide basic accounting and other information to Parliament and to the public. This reflects the fact that they are funded by the public and directly or indirectly accountable to the voters.

Beyond legal obligations, the amount of information that organisations are willing to disclose varies a great deal. Most private companies release only the minimum level of information to outsiders. But they often supply more detailed accounts to key shareholders who

Key term

Limited liability means that the owners of a business are able to limit their responsibility for any losses incurred by the business, i.e. to the value of their investment.

47

may also be directors and managers. The law demands that public limited companies (plcs) disclose far more information to the public. This is because their shares are not bought through private arrangements but in an open market. Large numbers of shareholders will never meet the directors or vote on how to run the business. Their interests therefore need protecting through an adequate flow of information about how the directors are managing the company on their behalf. However, the financial information supplied is still a summary and does not usually include any detailed insight into the company's strategy.

Business enterprise affects everyone and everyone is involved in business enterprise in some way. Most people have multiple connections with the business world. These can be grouped together according to the nature of their relationship with business.

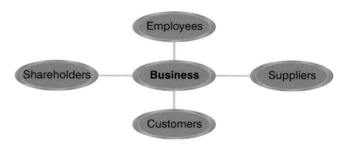

Figure 5.46 Business connections

Understandably, people connected through each of these relationships want information to further and protect their interests.

ACTIVITY

Figure 5.47 Different groups may have an interest in a leisure centre

The Leisure Centre opened in 1984 under the ownership and control of Lashford District Council. Although it was successful at first, it began to decline because a larger and better equipped centre opened ten miles away. Meanwhile financial cuts forced the Council to delay repairs and by 2001 the main building looked tatty and some of its facilities were out of use.

It was therefore a surprise when First Leisure plc proposed to the Council that it should buy the Leisure Centre with a promise to restore and upgrade its facilities.

Tasks

1 What kinds of information about First Leisure plc might the Council require?
2 The Lashford Gazette (the local paper) aims to represent the community and its services. What questions might its reporter put to a representative of First Leisure?
3 Who might want information from First Leisure about its proposed acquisition of the Leisure Centre?

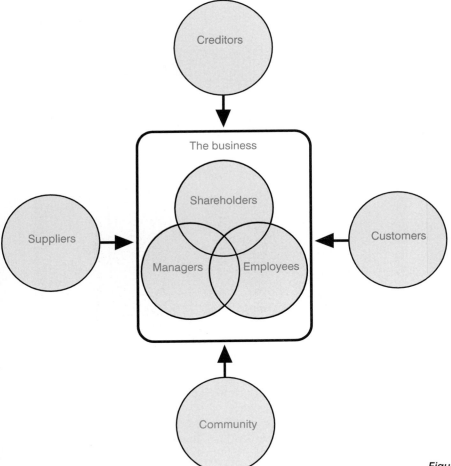

Figure 5.48 The stakeholder model

The claims of the interest groups are most effectively analysed through use of a stakeholder model. This highlights the groups of people with a 'stake' in the firm's performance and behaviour.

In Figure 5.48, the inner groups have a strong stake in terms of ownership or power or both. These are the groups that can be held most directly responsible for the firm's actions. However, it is important to remember that private shareholders, although they are strictly 'owners', may have a very small stake in the business and wield very little influence over its decisions.

The outer groups of stakeholders usually have no formal 'say' in the affairs of the firm. They are still stakeholders because they are affected – often vitally – by the decisions of directors and managers. The availability of financial information to these outer stakeholder groups is very important if they are to make fair or useful judgements on the company's affairs.

CTIVITY

Figure 5.49 *The end of the mine: South Crofty, Cornwall*

It is very rarely that a business activity ends when it has been running for some 3,000 years. But on 8 March 1998 the closure of South Crofty mine at Redruth in Cornwall marked the final end of tin-mining in Britain – and Europe. The industry had been declining for a long time and South Crofty was the last survivor. Before it closed it employed 135 men in an area of low wages and high unemployment.

The mine had been purchased by a Canadian company, Crew Developments, in 1994 from Rio Tinto. Barely profitable, it was then hit

by a falling world price for tin. Meanwhile the pound increased in value.
Since tin is sold on the world market in dollars, this meant that fewer pounds
were received by the company for every dollar in sales.

Tasks

1 Which stakeholders might have wanted access to financial
information from Crew Developments?
2 In what sense did the miners' trade union have a 'stake' in South Crofty?

There are many reasons why the stakeholders outside the firm's
ownership and management might want financial information.
Employees may be represented by a trade union or may belong to a
company-based staff association. Some firms operate consultation
systems which give staff representatives an opportunity to make their
point of view felt in the discussion process. Effective trade union or staff
participation in decision making depends on access to information in
general and financial information in particular. Some firms refuse to
disclose key data but others share some confidential information with
trade union or other staff representatives.

Creditors and suppliers may only be willing to lend or to supply
products on credit if they have access to the relevant financial
information. Major trade creditors will want to check the firm's solvency
and underlying stability. When considering loans, banks normally expect
to get detailed accounting statements and budgetary information as well
as full business plans. From the standpoint of creditors, limited liability
represents a risk. If the company collapses or enters receivership, there is
no guarantee of being repaid. Creditors therefore want hard evidence of
solvency and profitability and may require some form of security. This
entails part of the firm's fixed assets being legally committed for the
repayment of a debt in the event of default. Should the firm default on
its debt (fail to repay), then the secured asset is sold and the proceeds
used to repay the creditor.

 Limited liability, page 47

Community representatives have many reasons for wanting access to
a firm's accounting information. The local council may want to assess
council tax liability. It could also be concerned to evaluate the
company's long-term prospects. Will new jobs be created? Will land be
wanted for industrial use? How will transport needs be met? Is there a
risk of the firm relocating or even closing?

Organisations that campaign for such causes as environmental
protection will also be keen to assess accounting information. A pressure
group of this kind would also be especially interested in the
environmental reports that many leading public companies now produce.

Finally the government also has an interest in firms' financial
reporting. All kinds of statistical information about business is collected
by the Office for National Statistics (ONS). Firms making applications

Key term

An **environmental report** (often
published once a year) explains a
firm's policies regarding their impact
on the natural environment. It may
set targets for future impact and
evaluate performance in meeting
targets since the last report.

for financial help, when planning to locate activities in areas of high unemployment, must provide detailed accounting information. Meanwhile the Inland Revenue will want complete accounts in order to assess a company's tax liability.

Limitations of ratios

Although balance sheets form the raw material of ratios, there are some important criticisms to be made of balance sheets. In a sense the balance sheet is a snapshot of the firm with some important parts missing. Back in the nineteenth century, when modern accounting systems developed, the value of a typical manufacturing firm really was centred on its fixed assets and stock. But today many firms are worth far more than the valuation of net assets that appears on their balance sheet.

One way to measure the market value of a public company is to calculate its capitalisation:

Number of shares issued × share price = Capitalisation

CASE STUDY

ARM plc

Established in 1990, ARM (Advanced RISC Machines) produces the designs or 'architecture' for microprocessors. Based in Cambridge and working with major manufacturers around the world, ARM technology is found, for example, in mobile phones, palmtops, satellite decoders, cameras, printers, faxes and modems.

	£m	£m
Fixed assets		28
Current assets	100	
less		
Current liabilities	26	
Net current assets		74
Net assets*		102
financed by		
Shareholders' funds		102
Capital employed		102

*ARM's long-term liabilities were negligible.

Figure 5.50 Extract from ARM's report and accounts

A capitalisation value gives an idea of a company's true worth. But because share prices change constantly, capitalisation can rise or fall by a large margin in one day. Indeed, when one firm is considering a takeover bid by buying another company's shares, it usually offers a price that is well above their recent average value. It is not surprising that even the rumour of a bid can cause a dramatic rise in the share price of the target company.

At Psion the most valuable assets are:
1 the senior management
2 the company research and design teams
3 accumulated knowledge and experience
4 the brand name and reputation.

As none of these assets appear on the balance sheet we do not get a true value of the firm's worth. In reality ARM's capitalisation is about 25 times greater than the value of its 'official' net assets. This means that Return on Capital Employed (ROCE) has limitations as a measure of efficiency. In calculating ROCE we usually use the wider definition of capital employed, i.e. equity plus long-term liabilities or all long-term capital in the business. But if the resources on the balance sheet are only part of the full story, then is ROCE a satisfactory ratio? We can probably say that it is an indicator of efficiency and is certainly useful when comparing values for one year against another.

Window dressing

When the directors of a company publish their accounts, they try to make a good impression. This is particularly important for a public company with a Stock Exchange quotation. Shareholders need to be kept satisfied and the share price is likely to be higher if prospects seem good. Future share issues are also more likely to attract investors if the firm seems to be doing well. A company that presents its accounts legally but with the intention of giving a favourable impression is said to be window dressing.

There are many ways of giving a 'shine' to published accounts. For example, stock can be given a boost or a dip in value by choosing a balance sheet date that regularly sees stock levels at their highest or lowest (e.g. before or after Christmas). Alternatively, fixed assets can be kept down by ensuring a brisk rate of depreciation. Equipment, the book value of which is near zero, may still be in productive use. This all helps to strengthen the ROCE percentage.

> ### Key term
> **Window dressing** means the lawful presentation of accounting data with the intention of giving a more favourable impression of the firm's affairs than is necessarily justified.

| Budgeting

What is a business trying to achieve? What does it want to have achieved a year from now? What is its goal for the coming month? These are important questions because their answers guide decision making throughout the enterprise. A business enterprise has both aims and objectives. Aims are statements of direction while objectives are intended points of arrival.

The aim of a small business may only be 'to make a living' or even 'to survive'. But it will still have objectives such as a monthly value for total sales. Larger companies often have very broad aims such as long-term profitability or continuing expansion. Their objectives might include doubling sales to continental Europe or building a 5 per cent share in a new market.

ASE STUDY

Tesco plc

'By understanding customer needs better than anyone, we aim to increase value for customers, earning their lifetime loyalty and to enhance returns to shareholders.'

Source: Annual Report and Financial Statements 1999

Cadbury-Schweppes plc

'We have set three financial targets to measure our progress:
1   to increase our earnings per share by at least 10 per cent each year
2   to generate £150 million of free cash flow every year
3   to double the value of our shareowners' investment within four years.'

Source: Annual Report 1998 (setting targets for 1998–2002)

The achievement of objectives depends on the use of resources. Since resource movements are expressed in terms of financial information, it follows that objectives imply some financial planning. Put a different way, the business must be steered towards its objectives and this is likely to involve clear intentions for:
- sales
- output
- costs (direct and overhead)
- liquidity and cash flow
- capital spending (e.g. purchase of equipment)
- personnel
- profit.

A statement of financial intentions for the year ahead is called a budget. A budget is a series of financial plans (usually computerised) broken down on a monthly basis. Large firms use customised software but small enterprises often find off-the-peg programs adequate. Again a budget for a larger firm may form part of a longer term plan (e.g. to move up-market) that is spread over 3–5 years.

Budgets have a number of business functions. They:
- provide a framework for the process of planning performance to match objectives
- motivate staff towards meeting agreed targets
- ensure a structure for financial control within the organisation.

Managers normally have a budget to cover the financial flows for which they are responsible. In larger firms these defined areas of responsibility are classed as:
- cost centres, which are any convenient sub-divisions of an organisation that are a significant source of financial cost, e.g. a group of plastic injection moulding machines or the marketing department
- profit centres, which are sections of the business allowed to operate like enterprises in their own right and make a profit (or loss), e.g. a coffee shop within a supermarket.

There are important human factors to consider in drawing up a budget. It should not be a rigid plan imposed by senior management. Instead, managers at all levels should be consulted and involved in the process of setting each budget. In this way staff are far more likely to feel a sense of commitment to the decisions that are built into their budget. Often a first draft is circulated, giving managers a chance to argue for changes where they see plans that conflict or appear unrealistic.

Budgets are usually drawn up for each operating unit within the firm. When these are all combined, they form a master budget which represents the next intended profit and loss account, balance sheet and cash flow statement. In this way the firm plans its next set of accounts and financial results. There is a risk of seeing this process as some magic formula for business success. But a firm can fail to meet its budget commitments or even be found to budget for relatively poor results.

The management at Booker, the largest cash-and-carry operation in the UK, were far from happy when announcing their 1999 results.

CASE STUDY

Booker Cash and Carry (now merged with Iceland freezer foodstores)

'Profits before tax and exceptional items for the fifteen months to March 1999 were £3.6 million compared with £76.1 million for the year ended December 1997 ... this performance was totally unacceptable to your Board.'

'The new Board and management team [knew] that expected profits for the year would result in a breach in banking [agreements], thus imposing a need to re-negotiate financial arrangements for the entire company.'

Source: Annual Report and Accounts, 1998–99

It is very important that budgets are realistic. They are not statements of ideal or even optimistic outcomes. Instead they should be achievable targets adopted with the intention that they will be achieved.

How do budgets work?

The pattern for budget data varies from one firm to another and will always be adapted according to need. We will use the example of a small firm with a limited product range.

CASE STUDY

Cotswold Kitchen Ltd

Cotswold Kitchen is a family business owned by Mike and Gill Hunt and their daughter Jess. The company produces a small range of high quality cakes to traditional recipes in a converted warehouse on the edge of Gloucester. The firm's main products are:

Cake	Average output/month
Farmhouse Classic	5,000
Cherry Orchard	7,500
Lemon Grove	3,500
Chocolate Log	4,000

The cakes are produced in batches over a six-day working week. Jess has taken over the marketing effort and now sells to small retailers, leading hotels, several wholesalers and one supermarket chain. Each cake is boxed and projects an image that is exclusive but rural and very 'English'. They are priced at £1.20 each.

Most budget statements are set out on a monthly basis with space for budgeted and actual results. We will look at a simple example of their sales budget.

Table 5.7 Cotswold Kitchen Ltd – Sales budget: January–March (units)

Product	January	February	March	Total
Farmhouse Classic	4,400	4,900	5,300	14,600
Cherry Orchard	6,900	7,200	7,800	21,900
Lemon Grove	3,100	3,600	3,900	10,600
Chocolate Log	3,800	4,000	4,300	12,100
Total Sales	18,200	19,700	21,300	59,200

This statement provides a basis for planning both production and marketing. It also gives the company an indication of likely staff requirements. When looked at over a longer period, budgeted sales may also indicate any need for investment in capital equipment (e.g. new ovens, mixing machines, etc).

During the financial year a key function of the budget is to allow comparisons between budgeted and actual sales. Let us focus on the month of March:

Table 5.8 *Cotswold Kitchen Ltd – Sales budget: March*

Product	Budget units	Actual units	Variance Units	%
Farmhouse Classic	5,300	5,486	+186	+3.51
Cherry Orchard	7,800	9,237	+1,437	+18.42
Lemon Grove	3,900	4,092	+192	+4.92
Chocolate Log	4,300	3,183	−1,117	−25.98
Total	21,300	21,998	+698	+3.28

Can budget data be used to investigate the source of failure?

The difference between budgeted and actual sales is called a variance. Since no budget can be exactly accurate, small variances are inevitable and usually not significant. But a key task of managers is to watch for variances that are unexpected – either in their size or timing. Adverse variances (unfavourable to the business) may suggest:

- unrealistic budgeting which may mean that the budget data should be revised or 'flexed'
- a failure with the firm (e.g. missed calls by salesforce); this needs immediate management attention
- a change in the external environment (e.g. a new competitor); this may suggest a counter-attack with increased marketing activity or a reblending of the marketing mix.

The idea that managers should concentrate their attention on events that are not in line with expectations – or management by exception – means that only routine attention is directed to events that are expected or in line with budget.

ACTIVITY

Cotswold Kitchen Ltd – March sales variances

Because orders from larger customers can fluctuate for many reasons, the company does not view variances of less than 10 per cent as likely to be significant. However, variances in the range of 5–10 per cent are considered as early pointers towards what may become a significant gap between

The 'exceptions' can then be treated rather like red lights on a control panel. Adverse variances attract management attention and prompt investigation into what has gone wrong. Favourable variances represent good news, but should not be ignored. Instead they carry an opportunity. Managers should first check whether their original budgeted date was overly cautious or pessimistic. If not, then perhaps a new market is emerging or a competitor has withdrawn. The goal, in any case, will be to make the favourable variance larger!

Significant changes may also be hidden beneath nil variances. This occurs when favourable and adverse variances cancel each other out. Perhaps the adverse variance can be eliminated?

budgeted and actual results. Variances over 10 per cent need urgent investigation.

The Farmhouse Classic and Lemon Grove are performing fairly close to budget, but why have sales of Cherry Orchard soared 18 per cent above budget? And why is the Chocolate Log performing so much below expectations? Both trends became noticeable after Christmas, but have now intensified. It is time to investigate.

Tasks

1   a) If the budgeted data for the Chocolate Log was in line with reasonable expectations, suggest possible causes for the unfavourable variance.
    b) For each reason given, suggest a possible response from the company's management.
2   An increasing number of hotels are becoming customers of Cotswold Kitchen.
    a) Why might the Cherry Orchard be selling so well?
    b) What kind of management action might now be a good idea?

| Cash flow and working capital

We have seen that the balance sheet is like a snapshot of the firm at a given moment in time. This means that it is an attempt to identify the origin, use and value of all the resources in the firm. These fall into two types:

- *fixed assets* that remain in the business and assist the process of adding value over the longer term
- *current assets* that are drawn through the business as sales of the product take place.

In order to generate sales revenue, a business has to incur costs. This is equally true of manufacturing and service enterprise. As a firm uses resources, so it becomes liable to pay the bills or debts that follow.

When you buy a product in a shop, you momentarily incur a debt. It only lasts for a few seconds before you settle the bill. In running a business, many debts are incurred but there is usually a longer time lapse before they are settled.

The profit and loss account summarises the payments that a firm has met during a trading period. For a manufacturing business these might typically include:

Table 5.9 Some costs of running a business

Profit & loss account heading	Typical subject of payment
Sales revenue	
Cost of materials	Raw materials, components
Cost of labour	Wages
Gross profit	
Marketing expenses	Advertising, promotions, distribution
Administrative expenses	Rents, rates, salaries
Operating profit	
Interest charges	Interest to banks and other lenders
Profit before tax	
Tax	Tax payable to the Inland Revenue
Profit after tax	
Dividends	Dividends payable to the shareholders
Retained profit	

It is extremely important that a business can meet its debts. Any significant failure could at best damage the firm's reputation and at worst trigger legal action and possible liquidation.

When a firm is said to be 'bust' or 'bankrupt', this is not literally true but it does normally mean that the business is insolvent or unable to pay money owing. A company may then move into receivership on a voluntary basis or by court order. This means that the affairs of the business are taken over by the Official Receiver (a government official) who will liquidate (i.e. sell) the business's assets in order to repay as much of its debts as possible.

Remaining solvent means ensuring that sufficient cash is always available or quickly obtainable. You might therefore think that a business wants to keep large sums of cash ready to meet every need. This is not the case. Holding cash earns the business little or no income. Only when resources are held as value-adding assets can they generate worthwhile returns. After all, the whole purpose of an enterprise is not to store money but to make it work in the business. So cash is very necessary to ensure solvency but carries a real opportunity cost.

The answer lies in a compromise. The firm must ensure that it has enough cash to trade safely but not so much that the opportunity cost is unacceptable.

In what form should the cash be held? Literal, petty cash is only ever kept in the smallest amounts. It earns nothing and represents a security risk. Cash at the bank is readily available and may earn a little interest. Many firms also have an overdraft facility which enables them to borrow on demand while only paying interest on the amount outstanding.

Then there are the other assets of the firm that have a cash value. The issue here is their *nearness to cash* or liquidity. Current assets include cash

 Solvency, page 41

Key term

Receivership means that responsibility for a company's affairs has passed from the board of directors into the hands of the Official Receiver who will act in the interest of the firm's creditors.

 Opportunity cost, page 6

and are the nearest to cash – or the most liquid. Debtors will normally pay their bills and are the next-most-liquid asset after cash itself. Many firms, especially smaller ones, use debt factoring facilities. This means that the debt factor (such as International Factors owned by Lloyds TSB) pays the firm immediate cash for a high percentage value of its outstanding trade debtors. Further payment will be received when the debt is actually settled but obviously the debt factor makes a charge for the service.

Stock is the next most liquid asset but its cash value is often uncertain and may be reduced by any need for quick sale. It is conservatively valued on the balance sheet at cost or net realisable value, whichever is the lower. Net realisable value simply means the amount for which it could readily be sold after allowing for any costs involved.

ACTIVITY

Beetle Mania

It is January, and Ross Bradford and his brother-in-law Andy are starting their second year of running Beetle Mania as a profitable part-time job. It all began when Ross bought a VW Beetle through an ad in the local paper. 'Clean and reliable' it had said. Actually the car was filthy and always breaking down. In getting it roadworthy Ross learned a lot about Beetles. But it was Andy's girlfriend Sophie who suggested buying 'dodgy' Beetles advertised in the local paper, doing them up and selling them at a profit. On average each car has cost £1,000 with about a month elapsing between purchase and sale.

In order to reduce the need for working capital, the cars have generally been bought one at a time, although to keep up the flow of work the next car is generally bought before the current one is finished. Sometimes their bank overdraft facility of £1,000 has been useful. So far a total of 16 Beetles have passed through Sophie's father's garage where they do the work. Now Andy has been offered the chance to buy four cars at once.

'It's a collector who can't afford the repairs,' he explained. 'We can get all four for three grand and laugh all the way to the bank.'

Balance Sheet as at 31 December 2000

	£	£
Equipment		2,500
Stock	1,000	
Debtors	500	
Cash	2,000	
Creditors	1,250	
Net current assets		2,250
Total assets less current liabilities		4,750

Bank loan	2,000
Owners' funds	2,750
	4,750

Figure 5.51 *Beetle Mania Ltd*

Tasks

1 On the evidence available, do you think Ross and Andy have enough working capital to buy the four cars? Explain your view.
2 What steps might they take if they want to expand their business? Give reasons.

FIXED ASSETS
Land/buildings
Plant
Machinery
Fittings
CURRENT ASSETS
Stock
Debtors
Investments
Cash

Figure 5.52 *Spectrum of liquidity*

Fixed assets are less liquid: buildings and machinery cannot easily or quickly be turned into cash. Generally the firm's assets are shown on the balance sheet in ascending order of liquidity with cash listed last.

The degree of liquidity within a firm is measured by the current ratio and by the more demanding acid test ratio.

 Current ratio and acid test ratio, pages 41–42

 **ASE STUDY**

	Tate & Lyle Plc		Tesco plc	
	£m	£m	£m	£m
<u>Current assets</u>				
Stock	479		744	
Debtors	535		252	
Investments and cash	261	1,275	346	1,342
Sales		4,090		20,358
Total assets less current liabilities		2,165		6,382
<u>Current liabilities</u>				
Creditors		964		3,487
Net current assets/ (liabilities)		311		(2,145)

Figure 5.53

Tate & Lyle has a fairly conventional current ratio (1.32). Its acid test ratio is 0.83, which suggests fairly safe coverage of current liabilities.

Tesco is a complete contrast. As a supermarket chain, the business has a faster asset turnover (at 3.2 against Tate & Lyle's 2.0) and achieves very high sales with relatively small current assets.

The company also trades with negative working capital (net current assets) and very low liquidity ratios. This is quite normal in retailing because a firm such as Tesco pays its suppliers well after the receipt of goods, meaning a high value in creditors.

 Asset turnover, page 39

Profit or cash

Cash represents resources in a completely liquid form. By definition, cash can be used in exchange for resources in any other form. Sales create a flow of cash through the business. This can be used to meet the costs of future sales. Cash matters because it settles the indebtedness that arises from these costs. Profit is a surplus of sales revenue over cost. It represents a firm's success in selling output at a higher price than the cost of corresponding inputs. Profit need not be in the form of cash but may exist in the form of debtors, or promises of payment in the future.

ACTIVITY

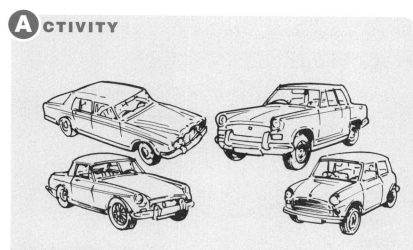

Figure 5.54 Car Classics Ltd

Gareth and Darren Peglar make miniaturised metal die-cast reproductions of famous British cars. Their turnover last year was £180,000 with 40 per cent gross and 20 per cent net profit margins. On 20 February Darren accepts an order from a department store for 1,000 models at £8 each. The store agrees to make full payment within 30 days of receiving the goods. Gareth estimates that delivery should be possible in six weeks' time.

Tasks

1 What is the projected gross profit on this order?
2 When would the company's accounts record a profit being made?
3 Suppose that the firm runs short of cash during April. In what ways could this order (a) not help; (b) help?

Want to know more?

While cash is the most liquid form in which resources can be held, profit is an accounting surplus. The difference becomes clear when applied in context.

Car Classics Ltd

Profit but no cash?	Cash but no profit?
Darren attends an international show in Hanover. A large German retail chain is prepared to buy 10,000 models at the usual price with more orders promised.	It is February and trade is very slow. Stocks are building as orders fall. Bills continue to arrive and Darren is increasingly worried about the company's dwindling cash. Reluctantly he accepts an offer to purchase 500 models at half price.
Gareth is all for expansion with a new workshop, more machinery and a proper office. A loan offered by the bank, he argues, will cover at least half the cost. But their accountant advises scaling down the order as her projections show the company running out of cash before sufficient sales revenue is received.	'But that's making a loss,' complained Gareth. The models cost us £5 each when you include all our costs.

'Yes, but we need £2,000 in cash. Now.' Darren shrugged. |

Planning cash flow

Every business must aim to make a profit or surplus in the long run. It is not the aim of business to generate cash for its own sake. But in the practical operation of a business, cash is indispensable. At best, lack of cash will constrain and distort decision making. But at worst it may endanger the whole business with the prospect of insolvency and receivership. It is not surprising that among business people it is often said: 'Cash is king'!

It is therefore a basic task of financial managers to anticipate the cash needs of the business and to plan the inflows and outflows of cash in the trading period ahead. The tool for this purpose is the cash flow forecast. For each month (or other interval) of the period covered it estimates the inward and outward flows of cash and the resulting cash balance at the bank.

CASE STUDY

Noah's Ark

Clare Kego makes a range of porcelain animals from plaster moulds. When they have been fired in her kiln she hand paints them and sells the finished products in specially designed presentation boxes. During the summer she builds up stock as she makes over half her sales in the months leading up to Christmas. The situation this year is looking difficult since she has spent most of her cash balance on a new kiln. Clare pays herself £12,000 per year and pays an assistant Nick £500 per month over busy periods. Her material costs amount to 10 per cent of the sales value. Stock is held on average for two months. Overheads are quite heavy since she has to pay for trade stands at craft fairs and costly brochures.

Table 5.10 Cash flow

	Jul £	Aug £	Sep £	Oct £	Nov £	Dec £
Cash inflow						
Sales	2,600	1,800	3,400	5,500	8,100	7,900
Cash outflow						
Labour	1,000	1,500	1,500	1,500	1,000	1,000
Materials	340	550	810	790	220	130
Overheads	1,250	1,250	1,250	1,250	1,250	1,250
Net cash flow	10	(1,500)	(160)	1,960	5,630	5,520
Opening balance	400	410	(1,090)	(1,250)	(710)	4,920
Closing balance	410	(1,090)	(1,250)	(710)	4,920	10,440

It is clear that an overdraft facility will be needed from August, perhaps of £1,500.

▶ Budget, page 54

A best estimate of cash needs will be included in the firm's budget but it is also helpful to hold some reserve cash – or very liquid assets – to meet unexpected needs. In addition, large firms sometimes build 'cash mountains' as a deliberate strategy so that they have a 'war chest' with which to launch bids for other companies.

It is clear that a cash flow forecast helps a business to plan its cash needs and to address any problems before they become serious. However, the process of cash flow forecasting carries the danger of making what are forecast data appear like real data. A cash flow forecast is only as secure as the assumptions on which it is based. Some of these may be fairly safe, such as a surge in sales before Christmas. But others are much less certain. Will some new designs prove popular? Will material costs remain constant? Might there be a rent review? Could competition suddenly increase? What would happen if an economic downturn begins? These and many other questions can have no certain answers and the uncertainty increases as the business looks further into the future.

The use of spreadsheets in financial planning encourages managers to try exploring more and less favourable scenarios and to look at the possible implications. No business can eliminate risk from its activities but it can at least manage risk in an active and realistic way. Running short of cash is a particularly important risk to manage.

What causes cash flow problems?

Although almost any change in the circumstances of a business has the potential to affect adversely the pattern of cash flow, there are a number of well known causes:

- overtrading when a business tries to expand its sales value faster than its working capital will allow; this typically occurs when orders are taken that will be profitable in the longer term but require more cash than the firm can generate
- fluctuations in demand where sudden shifts in fashion or competition may cause surges and troughs in sales
- seasonal variation that may include periods of very low sales
- excess stockholding when a business maintains its output in the face of low sales with the expectation of orders to come
- problems in credit control when a business has difficulty in making sure that debtors settle their accounts within a reasonable time
- capital expenditure on fixed assets when optimism about the future leads to over-acquisition of property, equipment or vehicles
- excessive borrowing, leading to the burden of high interest charges
- emergencies that can arise in any business such as damage to stock, adverse publicity, legal action or major bad debts.

 Working capital, pages 30, 58

Tackling cash flow problems

Since cash is money and money represents resources, almost every aspect of a business is relevant to cash flow problems. Key areas for possible improvements in cash flow include the following.

Cash inflows

- Improve credit management with efforts to cut debtor repayment period.
- Negotiate shorter credit period with customers.
- Factor debts to obtain immediate cash.
- Sell selected stock at reduced prices in a 'sale'.

Cash outflows

- Arrange longer credit terms with suppliers.
- Reduce stockholding levels by slowing down production.
- Find ways to cut costs.

Capital inflows

- Sell off any surplus fixed assets.
- Use sale and leaseback of existing assets to obtain cash upfront.
- Postpone new purchases of equipment or lease rather than buy.

Obtain additional finance
- Agree a bank overdraft to cope with fluctuations in cash flow.
- Arrange a short-term loan to cover some cash expenses.
- Obtain a long-term loan to cover any new fixed assets.
- (For companies) issue and sell more shares.

Depending on the business and its circumstances only some of these solutions will be effective or appropriate. A financial manager must look at all possibilities and try to find the best combination of remedies for any cash flow shortfall.

 CTIVITY

Figure 5.55 Dream Ice Cream

Charlotte Weston and Dawn Evans first tasted locally made Cornish ice cream while on a surfing holiday at Newquay. Two years later they had a thriving ice cream business of their own near Poole in Dorset. As Charlotte often said, there was no lack of customers and they worked hard to supply retail shops, restaurants and hotels. But the seasonal nature of the business meant that cash flow was always a problem.

After an encouraging Christmas with good orders from a catering company, the difficult winter period lay ahead. Dawn made an estimate of sales for the next six months.

Table 5.11 Sales estimates

January	February	March	April	May	June
£6,500	£8,000	£11,500	£12,500	£16,000	£19,000

Wages for her and Charlotte would cost £4,000 every month while materials cost 30 per cent of sales value. Overhead costs were £1,000 each month and rose to £2,500 every March, June, September and December when the rent was paid.

Tasks

1 Construct a simple cash flow forecast for Dream Ice Cream to cover the period January–June.
2 How might the business overcome any problems that you have uncovered?

Index

Asset turnover ratio 39, 61
Accounting requirements 6
Accounting Standards Committee 7
Acid Test ratio 42, 61
Acknowledgement 13
Audit 10

Balance sheet 23–31
Budgets 53–57, 64

Cash book 19, 24
Cash flow 7, 15, 54, 58, 63–65
Competitive advantage 46
Credit note 16
Current ratio 41, 61

Debtors/sales ratio 40
Delivery note 14
Dividends 36, 45
Double entry 20–22

Earnings per share 46
Efficiency 37
Environmental report 51

Factoring 60
Financial accounting 7
Financial information 2, 4, 23, 47
Financial records 1
Financial Reporting Standard (FRS) 7

Invoice 15

Ledgers 21
Letter of enquiry 11
Liabilities 27
Liquidity 41, 43, 54, 59, 61

Management accounting 7
Management by exception 6, 57
Memorandum of association 31

Non-executive director 8

Opportunity cost 6, 15, 37, 39, 59

Paying-in slip 18
Petty cash 21
Price-earning ratio 46
Profit 2, 32, 62
Profit and loss account 6, 32–36, 58
Profit margin 4, 38
Purchase order 12
Purchases day book 19

Quotation 11

Ratios 37, 52–53
Real time information 5
Receivership 59
Registrar of companies 7
Remittance advice 16, 17
Research and development 35
Reserve account 32
Return on capital employed (ROCE) 31, 37, 43

Sales day book 19
Shareholders 28–29, 43
Shares 43
Solvency 41, 59
Source and use of funds 25
Statement of Standard Accounting Practice (SSAP) 7
Stock exchange 8, 43
Stock turnover ratio 39

Tax 35
Trade debtors turnover ratio 40
Trial balance 23

Variance 57

Working capital 30, 58, 63